JOURNAL OF THE AMERICAN PLANNING ASSOCIATION
Eugenie L. Birch and Peter D. Salins
Book Review Editors

Graduate Program in Urban Planning
Department of Urban Affairs
Hunter College of the City University
of New York
695 Park Avenue, New York, New York 10021

PRIVATE
INNOVATIONS IN
PUBLIC
TRANSIT

PRIVATE INNOVATIONS IN PUBLIC TRANSIT

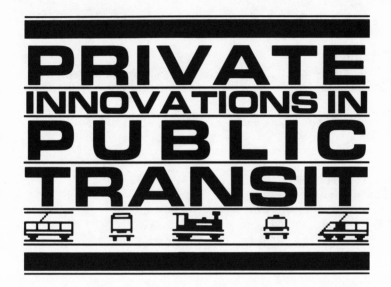

EDITED BY
JOHN C. WEICHER

American Enterprise Institute for Public Policy Research
Washington, D.C.

John C. Weicher holds the F. K. Weyerhaeuser Chair in Public Policy Research at the American Enterprise Institute. On a leave of absence from AEI during 1988, he is serving as associate director for economic policy at the U.S. Office of Management and Budget.

Distributed by arrangement with

UPA, Inc.
4720 Boston Way
Lanham, Md. 20706

3 Henrietta Street
London WC2E 8LU England

Library of Congress Cataloging-in-Publication Data

Private innovations in public transit.

   (AEI studies ; 468)
   Includes index.
   1. Local transit—United States. 2. Local transit.
3. Privatization—United States. 4. Privatization.
I. Weicher, John C. II. American Enterprise Institute
for Public Policy Research. III. Series.
HE4451.P74 1988   388.4′068   87-33667
ISBN 0-8447-3647-3 (alk. paper)

1 3 5 7 9 10 8 6 4 2

AEI Studies 468

Printed in the United States of America

Contents

Contributors

ROBERT CERVERO is an associate professor of city and regional plannig at the University of California, Berkeley, where he teaches land use planning, transportation, and computer modeling. He received his bachelor's degree from the University of North Carolina, master's degrees in engineering and in city planning from Georgia Institute of Technology, and his Ph.D. in policy and planning from UCLA. He is active in a number of professional societies and serves on the Committee on National Urban Policy of the National Academy of Sciences. Professor Cervero has published extensively on a range of urban transportation issues and is author of the book *Suburban Gridlock*. While on sabbatical leave from Berkeley, Dr. Cervero is conducting studies on rail transit in Europe and rural economic development in Indonesia.

WENDELL COX is an urban transportation consultant specializing in strategic planning, public policy analysis, competitive contracting, and transit organizational analysis. Mayor Tom Bradley appointed him to the Los Angeles County Transportation Commission in 1977, to which he was reappointed twice. While on the commission he led efforts to contain transit costs and to institute effective strategic planning. He served as chairman of two American Public Transit Association committees: Planning and Policy, and Governing Boards. In 1986 he became an independent consultant and has worked on a variety of projects including the Oakland County (Mich.) transportation study, the Urban Mass Transportation Administration–American Bus Association competitive contracting workshops, the private participation program of the Atlanta Regional Commission, and the Detroit transit reorganization program.

RONALD F. KIRBY is director of transportation studies at the Urban Institute in Washington, D.C. Educated in South Australia, Dr. Kirby has over fifteen years of research experience on transportation policy problems in U.S. cities. In addition, he has provided consultant services to the World Bank on transportation problems in Egypt, the Philippines, and other developing countries, focusing primarily on the regulation of unsubsidized, privately operated public transport services. His most recent work has dealt with the federal role in financing U.S. highways and mass transportation.

C. KENNETH ORSKI is founder and president of the Urban Mobility Corporation, a Washington-based consulting firm specializing in issues of public-private cooperation in transportation. He is a former associate administrator of the Urban Mass Transportation Administration (1974–1978), former vice-president of the German Marshall Fund (1978–1982), and former director of urban affairs and transportation at the Organization for Economic Cooperation and Development in Paris. He has written numerous articles and contributed to several books, including a study of private sector initiatives in transportation for *Meeting Human Needs: Toward a New Public Philosophy* (AEI, 1982).

JEFFREY A. PARKER is an adviser to government agencies, vendors, and investment banking firms on innovative capital investment strategies and the financing of private transit systems. He is active in an office development project in Pittsburgh that provides for a private people-mover system and has been an adviser on a similar system in Sydney, Australia. He has been on the staff of the U.S. Conference of Mayors and served as the youngest department director of the city of Pittsburgh.

JEROME C. PREMO has served as the first executive director of the New Jersey Transit Corporation (NJ Transit) since June 1980. He has initiated a capital program of over $1.5 billion to improve New Jersey's bus and rail network and has fostered a wide range of public-private partnerships in New Jersey, including a private bus industry support program. Before going to the Garden State, he served as executive director of the Los Angeles County Transportation Commission for three years. From 1966 to 1977 he was with the federal Urban Mass Transportation Administration, serving for five years as associate administrator for transit assistance. He is vice-president of government affairs for the American Public Transit Association.

PHILIP J. RINGO is chairman of the board and chief executive officer of ATE Management and Service Company, Inc., the largest transit management firm in the United States, currently managing fifty-five publicly owned U.S. transit systems. ATE also has a consulting practice, is minority owner of a short-line railroad, and operates twenty-two turnkey transportation systems. He is active in transit industry affairs, currently serving as cochairman of the American Public Transit

Association Task Force on Privatization. He is a graduate of Princeton University and the Harvard Business School.

JAY ROGERS is a senior associate with the International Center for Information Technologies (ICIT) in Washington, D.C. His work on this paper began while he was a senior associate with the Naisbitt Group working in their strategic design program. He has performed economic, political, and technology trend analysis for a variety of trade and professional associations, including a project on transportation trends for a major automotive manufacturer. Previously, Mr. Rogers worked as a Wall Street analyst, providing research for institutional investors, and has served as director of market analysis for the Pharmaceutical Manufacturers Association. He holds a degree in political science from Syracuse University.

GABRIEL ROTH, civil engineer and transport economist, is president of The Services Group, a nonprofit consultancy specializing in market-oriented approaches to economic development. During prior service at the World Bank, he worked on transit problems in many parts of the world, including Venezuela, Nigeria, Pakistan, Thailand, Malaysia, and Singapore. He has recently written *Private Provision of Public Services in Developing Countries* (World Bank, 1987) and is the coauthor of *Free Enterprise Urban Transportation* (Transaction Books, 1982).

JOSEPH P. SCHWIETERMAN is a strategic planning associate with United Airlines. He has written on the effects of regulation in the transit and airline industries, including a study of airline fares under deregulation for AEI's *Regulation* magazine and an analysis of subscription bus services in Chicago for *Reason* magazine. He holds an M.S. in Transportation from Northwestern University.

RALPH L. STANLEY is currently senior vice-president of the Municipal Development Corporation, a firm organized specifically to finance, design, own, and operate public facilities. He served as administrator of the Urban Mass Transportation Administration of the U.S. Department of Transportation from 1983 to 1987. As UMTA administrator, he oversaw the disbursement of over $4 billion per year to the nation's public transit systems. He previously served as chief of staff to former Transportation Secretary Elizabeth Dole and was special assistant for policy to her predecessor, Drew Lewis. He was an associate in the Washington law office of Bracewell and Patterson and was a financial analyst on Wall Street for the Bank of New York. He is a graduate of the Georgetown University Law Center.

ROGER F. TEAL is associate professor of civil engineering at the University of California, Irvine. He has studied numerous issues in public transit, including service contracting, private sector options for commuter transportation, and taxi-based services. He also has been a consultant to several local governments in the West and is a member of the Paratransit Advisory Committee of the Southern California Association of Governments. He has published widely in transportation journals.

GEORGE S. TOLLEY is professor of economics and member of the Committee on Public Policy Studies at the University of Chicago. From 1978 to 1985 he was director of the Center for Urban Studies at the university. He was deputy assistant secretary for tax policy and director of the Office of Tax Analysis at the U.S. Treasury in 1974 and 1975. He is coeditor of *Resource and Energy,* and he is a member of the Energy Engineering Board of the National Research Council. He has served as consultant to the ministers of planning of Venezuela and Panama, the Ministry of Agriculture of South Korea, the International Bank, and the Agency for International Development.

SIR ALAN A. WALTERS is a senior fellow at the American Enterprise Institute for Public Policy Research, professor of economics at Johns Hopkins University, and an economic adviser at the World Bank. He was personal economic adviser to Prime Minister Margaret Thatcher of Great Britain from 1981 until 1983, when he joined AEI. Previously he was the Sir Ernest Cassel Professor of Economics at the London School of Economics from 1968 until 1975 and has also taught at the University of Birmingham in England. He is a fellow of the International Econometric Society and is the author of several books on economics, money, and transportation.

JOHN C. WEICHER is currently serving as associate director for economic policy at the U.S. Office of Management and Budget, on a leave of absence from the American Enterprise Institute, where he holds the F. K. Weyerhaeuser Chair in Public Policy Research. He served as chief economist at the U.S. Department of Housing and Urban Development and has been a member of the Committee on Urban Policy of the National Academy of Sciences. His books include *Housing: Federal Policies and Programs* (1980) and *Maintaining the Safety Net: Income Redistribution Programs in the Reagan Administration* (1984), both published by AEI.

Foreword

Public transit in American cities faces increasing problems. Despite the much-discussed problems and frustrations of commuting, the number of people who drive to work continues to grow while the number of transit riders stays about the same from year to year. But as ridership remains unchanged, costs are rising. Fares now cover only about 40 percent of operating costs in public transit, down from 60 percent less than ten years ago, and down from 100 percent less than twenty years ago.

Rising costs in combination with growing fiscal pressures on government at all levels have allowed private enterprise gradually to assume a larger role in transit. In many large metropolitan areas— New York, Los Angeles, Chicago, Washington—private buses now carry thousands of passengers every day between the suburbs and downtown. In smaller metropolitan areas such as Phoenix and Nor-folk, local governments have contracted with private firms to provide bus service. This is not new; rather it is a revival of traditional transit policy. Before 1970 most urban transit services were provided by private companies. Only in the years since then have public ownership and operation become the norm and the nearly universal practice.

The American trend is also congruent with trends in other coun-tries. In Great Britain the government is throwing local transit service open to competitive bidding in a dramatic break with past policy. In many large cities in the third world, private firms provide transit, on both a regulated and an unregulated basis.

The trend toward private transit has coincided with, and to some extent has been reinforced by, a change in public policy at the federal level. The Reagan administration has sought to increase the private provision of transit services, building on and institutionalizing the trends of recent years. The administration has also attempted to eliminate federal operating subsidies for local transit systems. While it has not succeeded, it has nonetheless managed to cut operating subsidies by over 40 percent in constant dollars (20 percent in current dollars) from the 1981 peak of $1.1 billion.

In the summer of 1986 the American Enterprise Institute held a conference to discuss federal policy and local transit developments, with financial support from the Urban Mass Transportation Administration. This book contains the papers presented at the conference.

The papers cover a broad range of issues. C. Kenneth Orski, president of the Urban Mobility Corporation and a long-time analyst of public transit, describes the re-emergence of the private sector. Orski argues that the role of the private sector has changed. Traditionally, private firms operated transit systems under exclusive franchises, insulated from competition; today, they are selected on a competitive basis and subject to the discipline of the market. Private firms are also setting up their own mechanisms to address transit problems, as for example the transportation management associations, voluntary associations of developers and employers organized to deal with transportation issues, especially in suburban areas.

Federal policy efforts to promote privatization are described by Ralph L. Stanley, director of the Urban Mass Transportation Administration, and, from a local point of view, by Jerome C. Premo, director of New Jersey Transit. Stanley argues that public-private partnerships will become increasingly important as federal funding for transit declines, both for new fixed-rail projects and for improving existing systems, and that local transit authorities should be making provision for local private sector involvement in transit. Premo argues that federal concern with privatization has focused too narrowly on transit modes, though he notes that New Jersey contracts out bus service on certain routes. In his view, the whole range of functions carried out by transit agencies—payroll, maintenance, marketing—should be considered for potential privatization. Premo provides a perspective on the day-to-day problems of managing a transit system.

The financial problems of public transit have provided much of the impetus for renewed private involvement. Several papers focus on financial issues. Ronald W. Kirby, director of transportation studies at the Urban Institute, discusses a range of new financing sources such as development impact fees and road user charges. Toll roads are coming back into fashion, helped by new technology such as the electronic monitoring of congested roads, now in use in Hong Kong. Jeffrey A. Parker, a transit consultant, offers a taxonomy of innovations, distinguishing between financing mechanisms (public and private) designed to take advantage of federal tax laws and arrangements that share the economic benefit from new private developments such as impact fees, special assessments, and transferable development rights. He regards the former as undesirable and ultimately untenable, the latter as imperfect but preferable because they link transit to

xiv

activities that create economic value. Parker also argues that transportation planning and development are often divorced from economic reality and that systems are unnecessarily costly as a result. Jay V. Rogers, senior associate with the Naisbitt Group, describes innovations in privately funded transportation systems, as well as problems that have prevented private investment.

Contracting out for transit service is the focus of several papers. Roger F. Teal, associate professor of civil engineering at the University of California at Irvine, surveys science contracting. He distinguishes between franchise contracting, in which private firms operate a service "that has been pulled into the public sector in every way other than ownership," and competitive contracting, with firms winning bids to provide service for a few years, after which they must enter a new bidding cycle. His investigations of the cost savings from competitive contracting show that they vary with the size of the system. Small systems enjoy small percentage cost savings; large systems, larger savings. Teal reports a range from zero to 40 percent based on detailed cost models that he has developed, results consistent with his survey findings. He notes obstacles to contracting out: incentives for transit systems to maximize subsidies rather than seek to be cost-effective, and opposition from both labor and management.

Wendell Cox, transit consultant and former member of the Los Angeles County Transportation Commission, offers a similar analysis from a different perspective. He blames the structure of transit, a local service monopoly with no incentive to control costs, for the rapid rise in real transit costs since 1970 and argues for competitive contracting on the basis of cost-effectiveness. He characterizes the New Jersey policy as franchise rather than competitive contracting. Both Teal and Cox list success stories in competitive contracting: Yolo County in California; Snohomish County near Seattle; San Diego; Norfolk. Several of these services are provided by a firm headed by Philip J. Ringo, ATE Enterprises, the largest transit management firm in the United States. Ringo believes that the private role is growing and that major firms are being attracted into the industry. He argues that local public transit managers are facing the same economic pressures as the federal government and are beginning to respond in the same way. Perhaps unexpectedly, he argues that privatization is not a cure-all and the savings are often overestimated, "but 10 percent is fine with me."

Labor relations and labor costs are a recurrent theme in these papers. Much of the cost saving attributed to privatization results from lower wage rates or improved labor utilization. Premo graphically describes negotiations with the unions representing New Jersey

Transit workers. Cox notes the difference in wage rates between bus drivers for private firms and public transit systems and suggests bringing down the cost of labor by attrition, effectively guaranteeing jobs to present transit employees but filling new positions at more competitive wages. Teal points out that privatization is directly against the interest of the transit unions and their members. But Ringo states that the unions are less of a barrier to privatization than is commonly supposed and that private operation is not necessarily nonunion. Teal concludes that transit management is perhaps more of a problem than transit labor.

Several papers review and analyze examples of transit innovations in the United States and abroad. Robert Cervero, assistant professor of city and regional planning at the University of California at Berkeley, provides a summary of experience in U.S. cities, with a focus on the West Coast, where innovation seems more common and transit regulations have been modified more often to permit competition. The distinction between franchise and competitive contracting is often also a geographic distinction. Franchise contracting is the typical form of private sector involvement in the East, competitive contracting in the West and South. Cervero's paper is the only one not originally presented at the conference; it is updated and reprinted from *Regulation* magazine.

Joseph P. Schwieterman describes a private commuter rail service along an established commuter rail line in Chicago, again documenting cost savings but also noting service quality improvement from privatization. Schwieterman has written on transit issues in the Midwest.

George S. Tolley, professor of economics at the University of Chicago, considers transit innovation in a different perspective. He analyzes the likely changes in American transit if all subsidies and entry restrictions were terminated. He projects a small reduction in overall transit rides, less than 10 percent, but a very large shift among transit modes, with a substantial decline in bus and rail service, a small decline in taxis, and much greater use of jitneys and van pools. Tolley notes that a world without transit subsidies is often termed "unthinkable," and he does not expect subsidies to be eliminated in the immediate future. But his analysis is consistent with the innovations described by Cervero that are already occurring in many cities.

Finally, Sir Alan Walters, former economic adviser to Prime Minister Margaret Thatcher, describes current British initiatives, and Gabriel Roth, long-time transit policy analyst with the World Bank, reviews third world innovations. They broaden the discussion and indicate that American policy and practice are in many respects be-

xvi

hind other nations'. Walters describes the new British policy, competitive contracting of intracity bus service, which is attracting attention in America. Both Walters and Roth have participated in transit projects in many countries where private firms have an important transit role.

The subject of private innovation in urban transit fits especially well with AEI's long-established research and policy interests in the area of transportation policy. AEI's Center for the Study of Government Regulation has published major analyses of national transportation policy by such scholars as George W. Hilton, Paul McAvoy, John Snow, and James C. Miller III, and by policy makers such as John Barnum, deputy secretary of the Department of Transportation under President Gerald R. Ford. These studies have contributed to the policy discussions that led to the deregulation of the airlines, the trucking industry, and other transportation modes over the past decade.

AEI has also pioneered in the analysis of private roles in public policy. In 1982 AEI published the first major study of the roles of private groups in providing public services, a volume entitled *Meeting Human Needs: Toward a New Public Philosophy*, edited by Jack A. Meyer and including a chapter on urban transit by Kenneth Orski. Case studies of innovations in urban transit have been presented in AEI's *Regulation* magazine, among them the paper by Robert Cervero reprinted here. This volume is our latest contribution to the continuing public debate about transportation policy.

JOHN C. WEICHER

The American Enterprise Institute for Public Policy Research

Founded in 1943, AEI is a nonpartisan, nonprofit, research and educational organization based in Washington, D.C. The Institute sponsors research, conducts seminars and conferences, and publishes books and periodicals.

AEI's research is carried out under three major programs: Economic Policy Studies; Foreign Policy and National Security Studies; and Social and Political Studies. The resident scholars and fellows listed in these pages are part of a network that also includes ninety adjunct scholars at leading universities throughout the United States and in several foreign countries.

The views expressed in AEI publications are those of the authors and do not necessarily reflect the views of the staff, advisory panels, officers, or trustees. AEI itself takes no positions on public policy issues.

Part One

Overview

1
New Solutions to Old Problems in Public Transportation

C. Kenneth Orski

My purpose in what follows is to provide an overview of the re-emergence of private sector involvement in urban transportation. I stress the word *re-emergence* because we tend to forget that before the 1950s urban transit was largely in private hands, and most new roads were financed largely with private capital. Philosophically then, the so-called privatization is really nothing new.

The re-emergence of private enterprise is taking place under different conditions, however. Before the 1960s private transit companies operated under exclusive franchises and were effectively insulated from competition. In fact, they were insulated from competition just as effectively as the public transit systems that replaced them. Today, private providers are competitively selected and are subject to the discipline of the market. They can no longer behave like a regulated private utility. This new element of competition has, of course, had impressive effects on costs. Private contracting has experienced an impressive surge in recent years and constitutes one aspect of the movement toward greater private sector involvement in transportation.

The private sector is becoming involved in new areas—for example, private businesses and developers as well as employers are increasingly participating in traffic mitigation. The business community is being asked to assume some responsibility for the traffic problems their activities generate. This request is made on the good premise that the private sector is in a far better position than public agencies to influence commuters' travel habits. Public agencies are very good at appealing to our sense of civic responsibility, but they are not terribly good at creating incentives to change travel habits.

Businesses do have a set of incentives at their disposal. They can set aside preferential parking for car pools, they can provide subsidies to employees for transit, they can institute variable work hours, they can sponsor various shuttle services and, importantly, they can

3

charge for parking in private facilities—something that the local government cannot do.

So, increasingly, private participation is considered essential to the success of any traffic mitigation program. And a growing number of jurisdictions are now using negotiations and ordinances to bring the private sector into this increasingly important activity of alleviating or mitigating traffic in crowded suburban areas.

Transportation Management Associations

Another difference between the old private sector involvement and the new one is that today the private sector is creating its own instrumentalities and mechanisms to support its involvement in transportation. I have in mind the so-called transportation management associations (TMAs), which are voluntary coalitions of developers and employers, organized to deal with common transportation issues. The TMAs are particularly prevalent in suburban centers that are poorly served by public transit or are entirely beyond the reach of public transit.

Some twenty of these private TMAs already exist, and at least a dozen more are being launched. The intent of these associations is to provide a mechanism for the private sector to step in and provide supplementary transportation improvements and transportation services that local government cannot effectively provide.

The TMAs respond to an institutional vacuum that is often present in newly developing suburban areas. Tyson's Corner, Virginia, in suburban Washington, D.C., is a classic example. Indeed, the Tyson's Transportation Association was one of the country's first TMAs.

The TMAs are freewheeling and entrepreneurial, and because they are private entities they are unhampered by the usual bureaucratic constraints. They do not have to seek approvals at many levels, and they are able to devise solutions that would be difficult to effect in the more conservative environment of local government. So they may be ideally suited to dealing with the complex challenges of suburban mobility.

One important function of the TMAs, in addition to providing services and managing demand, is to serve as an advocacy instrument. The Tyson's Corner TMA has been extremely influential in lobbying at the county level for local transportation improvements.

Other TMAs have become influential by appealing directly to state legislatures. In fact, advocacy may emerge as the most important function of a TMA.

Some TMAs are also negotiating with public transit authorities for changes in service. The TMA in Dallas, for example, is going to negotiate with DART (Dallas Area Rapid Transit) for significant changes in the route structure that would better serve Dallas's suburban centers.

Private Developers' Contributions for Public Roads

Financing is potentially the most important area for private sector involvement. By now, the principle of requiring private contributions to fund the cost of highway improvements has become conventional wisdom. Developers are almost routinely asked to participate in the funding of highway improvements in at least a dozen states, among them California, Colorado, Texas, Florida, New Jersey, Pennsylvania, Maryland, and Virginia.

The intent is to shift some of the cost of transportation infrastructure from the general public to those whose actions have made the improvements necessary in the first place. And while some people, have likened the process of bargaining with developers to extortion (public officials call it *"enlightened* extortion"), no one denies that negotiations with developers have become an accepted part of the land development process.

Developers have also become a rich source of funds. In Fairfax County, Virginia, developers have committed over $80 million to road improvements in the past five years alone. In California the estimate is close to $180 million. And in one area, West Los Angeles, impact fees are expected to generate $235 million over the next twenty-five years.

And this is only the beginning. In the coming years, as federal dollars become even scarcer, developer contributions may become the chief source of financing of local highway improvements, almost certainly exceeding the revenue derived from general obligation bonds. If that seems somewhat farfetched, consider that in Fairfax County developer contributions over the past several years have amounted to more than half of the $134 million bond issue that was voted in December and that will be repaid over a period of twenty-five or thirty years.

In other words, in the past five years, private developers have contributed more than half of the amount that will be financed by the taxpayers over the next thirty years.

Toll Roads and "Privatized" Roads

The second trend in financing that I would keep a close watch on is toll financing. After years of languishing in semi-obscurity, toll roads are reemerging as a serious fiscal alternative. I need not say a lot about it, because we live in an area where a toll road has been a living example of the potential of toll financing. I am referring, of course, to the Dulles Toll Road. Traffic on the toll road has been virtually double the expectations just three years ago.

So toll roads have become once again a fiscal reality. They are staging a comeback because the application of toll financing is being used primarily for commuter highways rather than for interstate highways.

For interstate roads, tolls may not necessarily be an economic proposition; it costs almost twice as much to build an interstate highway today than it did, say, a decade ago, while revenues from tolls on an interstate highway have not come close to doubling. On the suburban highways, however, traffic has increased so much that tolls could become a prime source of financing.

An intriguing variation on the toll road is the British government proposal for "privatized" roads. Under that proposal, private consortia would build highways with privately arranged financing and then be paid annual royalties based on actual road usage and on the amount of development generated by the highway. Payments would start when the road is open to traffic and continue for twenty-five years, after which the road would revert to the public.

The scheme would shift some of the financial risks and rewards from the public to the private sector and would protect the public from overruns and encourage a more efficient use of capital.

I wish I could report that these privatized roads have been a huge success. The last I heard, however, the proposal had been dropped. As I understand it, the private sector demanded certain guarantees which, in the view of the British government, took the risk out of what was intended to be a risk venture. So that may be the end of privatized roads. But toll roads, I think, *are* a reality.

Private Transit Financing

Private financing of transit is less advanced than private financing of highways. Before the 1970s most transit systems did get financing through general obligation bonds. But in recent years, the financial condition of public transit has been such that transit authorities cannot get the investment grade credit rating needed to float their own bonds.

In that sense, transit systems find themselves in very much the same situation as public hospitals. Public hospitals have been virtually excluded from the revenue bond market because the private investment community places almost no value on the state and local subsidies when it assesses the financial carrying capacity of a hospital. The reason is that there is no guarantee that funds will be appropriated every year. And the same argument applies to transit. Public transit has been effectively cut off from access to the private capital markets. The one available illustration of interest by the private investment community in financing transit is the New York Metropolitan Transportation Authority (MTA), which has successfully marketed a $250 million bond offering secured solely by farebox receipts.

What allowed the New York MTA to execute the transaction is the unique place that transit occupies in the political and economic consciousness of the city. The financial community, which lives, or at least works, in New York, concluded that the subway system is too essential to New York's economy to be allowed to go bankrupt or to stop running. So they went along with financing of the MTA bond issue.

Whether farebox revenue bonds can be used by other transit systems remains to be seen. So far, to my knowledge, no other public transit authority has been successful in floating revenue bonds, which says something about the value the financial community places on public transit in other metropolitan areas.

I do have a final thought on the question of private financing of rail. If developers have a choice, they will spend their money on highways rather than rail. As highways become more congested, however, and as it becomes more and more difficult to push new highways through established areas, developers may have more incentive to finance rail access, especially if they can hook up with an already existing, well-developed rail system. Japanese developers, for example, have built rail lines that hook up with the existing Tokyo, Osaka, and Nagoya transit systems. They pay only the marginal cost of providing that five-mile segment that will link their community to the metropolitan rail transit system.

In a sense, a Dulles–Washington link would do the same thing. It would not be a separate line from Dulles Airport to Washington. It would hook up with the Metrorail system. There may be something to the idea of the private sector's simply adding small increments of rail lines that expand the outreach of the metropolitan rail network.

Part Two

New Approaches to Managing Public Transit

2
Privatization and the Challenge of Urban Mobility

Ralph L. Stanley

The notion of "privatization" in public transit is controversial, partly because the term has a different definition for everyone who uses it. It is important for two reasons. First, the role of the federal government in transit is declining. This is clear from the budget of the Urban Mass Transportation Administration (UMTA) for the past four or five years. The budget debate over UMTA has become the occasion for a basic policy battle, and the budget trend has been down. Nobody is talking about increased funding. Second, urban mobility is one of the greatest problems facing our cities. I cannot name an area more in need of new ideas or innovative proposals than urban mobility.

These two trends demand not just a discussion of what sort of dollars-and-cents assistance the federal government can provide, but what kind of innovative solutions we can adopt. That demand has led us to the concept of privatization, or public-private partnerships. At UMTA we are directing our efforts toward reducing barriers to these partnerships. In the successful systems of the future, some kind of public-private partnership will be a critical element.

Capital Costs

The capital cost of contracting is one of the barriers to private sector involvement that we hope to lessen. A public operator's capital costs, for example, are reduced 80 percent through federal grants. We are now developing policies in UMTA to make the capital portion of a private operator's contract eligible for the 80 percent federal funding. It is an effort to encourage private sector involvement and reduce the barriers that have inhibited many specific projects.

Our last reauthorization proposal included a number of provisions to enhance competition. In framing the rhetoric of this debate, I have avoided the term "privatization" because of some fundamental misunderstandings, one of which was that we were mandating a

11

certain percentage of private sector contracts to go to private companies. Instead we now talk about "competition."

We are encouraging competition in every way, shape, and form. To that end, our reauthorization stipulates that private operators be involved in the planning process. We were looking for private representation on transit boards, and we now have in legislation a minimum amount of service to be put out for competitive bids, a percentage that graduates upward.

That requirement, of course, generated a lot of opposition and controversy, as well as a lot of discussion. We worked very closely with representatives of both sides of Congress in the authorizing committees to ensure a workable compromise: local authorities are required to have in place a local private enterprise involvement program and some companion language to the effect that the level of private involvement at the current time is not a condition for grant approval. We are not specifying that a certain amount of private involvement must occur prior to providing a grant. I have tried to make that second point time and again; it was always part of the administration's proposal.

We also have been successful in coming up with a small, but growing, demonstration program involving actual examples of private sector involvement.

Capital Projects

I consider capital projects to have as much or more potential for private investment. If we at UMTA proceed with the three contracts for urban transit projects that Congress has "mandated"—in Seattle, Los Angeles, and Miami—those three contracts, if signed, would absorb $400 million, all of the new-start discretionary money through the year 1992. That, in effect, would freeze out all other cities currently looking at either bus way or new-start rail projects.

In the pipeline we have four projects in preliminary engineering that will cost $521 million in federal funds. In the next step, alternative analysis, we have ten projects at a total of about $3.1 billion. In systems planning, some thirty-five cities with fifty-two projects are considering some kind of fixed highway or major project at current rough estimates of about $12 billion in federal money and about $16 billion in total costs. Finally, the Washington Metro still has about a $1.4 billion federal share that is unfunded even with current authorizations. We are looking, then, at a total federal commitment expected to be about $19.5 billion with total costs on those projects of about $31 billion.

In my view, while this budget debate continues through the

Gramm-Rudman era, there is no way that these projects will proceed without much, much greater local and private sector investment. We can no longer assume the typical 75 percent federal investment on which so much planning was based.

We are very eager and willing to use the resources that do become available for us to fund some of these projects and to try to fill the gap in local or private sector funding on a last-dollar basis. That was our approach in Orlando, Florida, on a project on which the county has decided not to proceed. And again, that is the kind of approach we have followed on projects we are working on at Dulles Airport and on the west side of Manhattan.

The New York City Planning Commission will be the entity responsible for a lot of the zoning decisions on the development on the west side of Manhattan. Along this development route lie Columbia Presbyterian Hospital, the proposed television city that Donald Trump has on the drawing board, and the Convention Center, for which not one provision was made for parking. Madison Square Garden will move from where it is now over to a site on that line. There is another major consolidation occurring north of Battery Park. An enormous amount of development will occur, unconnected by anything other than the Seventh Avenue line, which is inconvenient and makes no sort of north-south sense.

Existing along that line is an old abandoned Conrail right-of-way buried in the highway days, and the state is willing to put that up at a dollar to the project. The developers are interested in setting up an assessment district, tax increment financing, or some way that will enable them to be the predominant financiers if they set up a bus way or light rail project along that corridor. The growth and density make it fit. This is the kind of project UMTA is trying to nurture. It makes a great deal of sense, and it has everyone's support. UMTA put about $1.4 million into a feasibility study with the Planning Commission with the idea that when the Planning Commission makes its decisions on development issues, it will get the developers to finance part of the construction of the line.

This project will happen. But given the yearly budget soap opera and the questionable feasibility, a lot of other projects I have mentioned are simply not going to happen, unless more creative kinds of financing approaches are taken. The projects will not be anything other than engineering dreams.

Local Public and Private Participation

At UMTA our aim with our discretionary funds is to match investment with a stable private or local financing base for projects on an

13

out-year basis. We are past the point in UMTA where we are able to begin any project without some strong fiscal and financial assurance that what we start will be finished. That creates an enormous challenge to people interested in these projects, forcing them not so much to choose a particular technology as to weigh the financing options and orchestrate the land use and development aspects of these projects before their construction. The protracted and animated public debate over land use around the stations recently opened on the Washington Metropolitan Area Transit Authority (WMATA) Orange Line is a case in point. Our efforts are to make those development decisions and associated choices at the time the stations are planned; it is simply backwards to have a local zoning debate on land use and development plans seven days before the opening of a $260 million investment as happened in Washington.

With the downward trend in financing from the federal government, the debate centers on how people with limited dollars can come up with a whole set of new solutions for solving these problems. My sense is that this issue is absolutely critical. Only those state, county, and local systems that come up with innovative combinations of public and private sources of funding to provide the service necessary will succeed.

Any transit authority in the country that can design a project with an innovative, entrepreneurial approach resulting in increased ridership, increased productivity, and increased mobility will find federal funding in a minute. The challenge is really urban mobility. We do not have a highway problem or a transit problem—it is a combination. I am constantly amazed when I visit cities where the parking problem is settled by the city parking commission, which has no dealings with the county, which is building a rail project but which in turn has no dealings with the state, which is principally responsible for roads.

I have never found a city that has set up the political structure to deal with a *mobility* problem as opposed to a transit or highway problem.

Every authority in every area is groping for the right combination of public and private investment in services that meets its needs. That will be our greatest challenge, a formidable one, as we try to devise domestic policy solutions at the federal level.

In the urban areas with a population of over a million, we should give a block grant for urban mobility and allow urban transit systems to go in with the state highway departments to come up with the best *mobility* solution.

The local political infrastructure, however, and the sort of pachinko machine that distributes federal transit dollars are not in place. All too frequently, of course, competing factions argue over their share, over distribution, and over responsibility.

The challenge to us all is to create innovative projects and solutions, based on competitive procedures, because we have passed the era of talking about public and private cooperation: we need to develop and put into place projects that work. Once we do that, the trend toward a real public-private combination in providing public services will be set for the years to come.

3
Privatization in Practice:
The Case of New Jersey Transit

Jerome C. Premo

New Jersey Transit is a public corporation with 9,000 employees, an operating budget of about $530 million for the fiscal year 1986–1987, and a major capital program. I like to think that New Jersey Transit reflects a changing approach to public management of public businesses. In this instance, it happens to be public transit. There is much more we can do to attend to the public business of public transit in a fashion that reflects a greater sensitivity to cost control, a greater ability to manage our public resources.

I say that not idealistically—although there is a streak of idealism remaining in me even after twenty years in public service—but rather because I have been fortunate enough over the past several years to be part of a unique governmental arrangement. I think there is a lot to be learned from New Jersey, just as we have learned from other states that have experimented in this arena. We are working with the private sector in a fashion that is as good as—and I would argue, more logical and appropriate than—any other place in the country. So I start from that perspective, although I am certainly willing to hear arguments to the contrary.

Contracting Out and Public-Private Partnership

I think the federal government is barking up the wrong tree in focusing on contracting out bus service. But in discussions in New Jersey and, to a degree, in my capacity as the vice-president for government affairs of the American Public Transit Association (APTA), I have tried hard not to limit my attention to this seeming frenzy of contracting out of a selected number of bus routes, because we really should be engaged in the efficient management of public resources. New Jersey Transit is the first public transit agency in the country, to my knowledge, to adopt a meaningful contracting-out policy at the board level. We did that in May of 1986. It was no big deal

16

because it is a continuation of something we have been doing 1 many years. Five percent of our bus service in 1986–1987—both ne service and some of the service already operating—was put up for public bid. Based on our analysis of the London Transport experience, on our discussions with other authorities around the country, and on common sense, we are using an avoidable cost basis rather than the fully allocated cost basis that UMTA suggested we use.

Using a line-by-line model, we will focus on cost opportunities, particularly in low utilization lines, and identify services in that fashion.

As to what constitutes 100 percent of costs, the contracting-out policy adopted by our board was scrutinized by private carriers in our state for several months. I believe that they endorsed it privately but, for a variety of reasons not having anything to do, per se, with the cost-allocation model, were silent about it in the public meeting.

We are accepting bids for bus service between downtown Newark and our airport, and we are providing at no cost up to ten buses for that service. We expect to have a decision made and good bus service between downtown Newark and Newark International Airport operating by fall 1986. Newark Airport, by the way, now serves more people than either Kennedy or LaGuardia airports.

The focus on contracting out is part of a public-private partnership. I would argue that what NJ Transit is doing—providing buses at no cost to private carriers—needs to be replicated around the country to encourage and sustain private enterprise. We have provided $75 or $80 million worth of buses at no cost to private carriers over the past few years. And having acquired at our own cost the Grumman Flexible buses that New York pulled out of service, we are refurbishing 120 of them. And of that number, about two-thirds will be provided at no cost to private bus companies. We also plan, subject to some cooperation and help from the Urban Mass Transportation Administration (UMTA), to rebuild 500 more of these buses, 300 of which will go to private carriers at no cost to them.

This plan is separate from our commuter bus program under which we have already provided at no cost 220 buses, each worth $160,000, to private carriers, and we are buying about 400 more buses, of which nearly 200 will be provided at no cost to private carriers.

We provide a $160,000 bus for nothing, which obviously is a saving to the operator. That is real money being saved, capital not being expended, that is improving the financial condition of that operator. That does not mean we are sitting idly on the sidelines. In early 1986 we requested a $5 million grant from UMTA to help cover insurance costs for private operators.

17

For what it's worth, we take credit for the private bus miles. You are aware that UMTA formula money is allocated based on many different factors, including bus miles. So all the bus miles operated by private carriers in New Jersey result in NJ Transit's getting a certain amount of money. We set that money aside in the Private Carrier Capital Improvement Program fund and make that money available again to the private operators.

Compare, if you will, these activities with what is going on in Massachusetts. Massachusetts has purchased twenty-five commuter buses, which in seven years will be repaid by the private carriers. I say, Good for Massachusetts, but come on down to New Jersey and learn what's *really* going on in public-private partnerships.

About 35 percent of our commuter bus transportation is operated by private carriers. Of the 100 percent of buses operated by those private carriers in commuter service, about 90 percent have been provided by NJ Transit at no cost to the carriers. So how much of the commuter service beyond the 35 percent now in private hands is possible? We're not sure. We are focusing less on the interstate system than on the intrastate, localized service. We operate in twenty of our twenty-one counties. What we want to do is get under our belt, consistent with our labor contract, the 5 percent or so of service, and in particular any new service, and then see where we're going.

I have been concerned about the UMTA discussion of mandating the contracting out of 5, 10, 15, and 20 percent over the next four years. Let us try contracting out in this new world and see how we do this year, review it at our board level and in the body politic, and then see what we can do next year.

Labor and Privatization

We do not try to duck labor issues, and I must say that we had some hearty discussion with our labor friends on all this.

But we are too narrowly focused when looking only at bus service. In my opinion, the real issue on Main Street, America, is how public transit funding, whatever its source, is going to be spent. We have argued that the whole range of business functions carried out by public transit agencies needs to be considered. And the men and women who make up transit boards in this country need to be actively involved in a debate, in a discussion, in an open forum assessing how much of the transit agency's budget is spent within the agency and how much is available for the outside world—whether it is contracting out of bus service or marketing or administrative services, including payroll.

I would note that one big issue that may make NJ Transit bus operations—the public bus operating unit within NJ Transit—extremely competitive in the contracting out of services, is the attitude of the union. Our union people are questioning some basic policies such as wage rates and hours of work. They are doing it in part because we negotiated a year ago a major part-time labor provision within our contract.

If we calculate savings, the fact of part-time labor is a new dimension that can make transit agencies, depending on how this part-time labor thing is played, extremely cost competitive. The policy question, the common sense question, is our objectivity and fairness in assessing sealed bids from private and public operators.

In the case of New Jersey Transit the issue that drew my attention to this more than any other was the fixing of escalators in our Penn Station. As part of a public-private partnership, we struck a deal for Penn Station in Newark under which private investors bought, in concert with us and Amtrak, that train station, which had been publicly owned. The government owned Penn Station; now three individuals own it. They do not own it for altruistic purposes. They own it so they can make a bundle under the tax laws.

Money drives decisions. The three men who now own Penn Station entered into a contract with New Jersey Transit using sale leaseback, and now we manage the station; we got a $15 million check, we put it in the bank, we are earning interest, and we are paying the cost of better security and cleanliness in that station for the next twelve years at no direct cost to the taxpayer. Of course, there is an indirect cost because these three private citizens got a tax break.

Before we took over the maintenance of Penn Station, Amtrak had its employees fixing the escalators. Two repair people were always on standby—even though the escalators didn't break down very often—and Amtrak was paying them to sit around looking at the escalators work. We said, Why don't we pay somebody when the escalators break down instead of paying somebody to watch them work? That's what contracting out is about, in my opinion. So we did battle. We had a major showdown with the union on that issue because it suggested to the unions something bigger—they saw what was coming down the road. After the five-week rail strike in 1983, New Jersey Transit instead of the unions came out managing the public system.

Having won the court battle over escalator maintenance, we gained the ability to negotiate within that very station. We then went to the union and said, Now that we have an escalator that works, we have to clean the station. We offered the union the opportunity to bid on the job, but reminded them that they would have to reduce their rates to get the contract. And would you believe, we now pay our union workers at Penn Station a 40 percent lower wage rate than we would have if we hadn't gone through the negotiating process.

It sounds great, but it's not completely, because we can't hold on to employees. They always want to move on to jobs that pay more. But it is better than paying 40 percent more unnecessarily. So from a management point of view, contracting out carries with it all sorts of headaches in the real world of management of a public function. Maybe running bus service is simpler than cleaning bathrooms.

Conclusion

My objective here is to communicate my support for a managed contracting-out process using avoidable costs as an approach. It is to communicate a desire to see a broadening of the contracting-out approach, from specific bus routes to provision of capital in support of "privatization."

Another of my objectives is to give the creative energies of the men and women who make up our transit boards the chance to zero in on the budget. How much of the budget is being spent in wages and other things internal to the agency? In our case, around 60 percent. The balance of that money is being spent on Main Street, New Jersey, America, on ad agencies, on laundries where they clean uniforms so we don't need to have a New Jersey Transit uniform division, on escalator repair in Penn Station, and on a lot of other things.

I have urged UMTA not to worry about the whole issue of bus service contracting for areas with fewer than a hundred buses. There's a reason for it.

To have a real impact, focus on where the bang for the buck is. And the bang for the buck is in areas with more than a hundred buses. Ninety-two percent of the expenses in this country in public transit are expended in those areas with over a hundred buses. We should see what kind of return we can get where most of the action is and then build on that.

Part Three

Financing Public Transportation

4
The Prospects for Greater Private Sector Involvement in Urban Transportation

Ronald F. Kirby

In a recent article the expression "the winds of change are blowing" was metaphorically applied to greater involvement of the private sector in urban transportation. Although we have indeed seen some promising developments in this regard, they are still quite limited, and many of us would like to see the winds blow a little stronger. The difficulty with the wind, of course, is that we have not yet learned how to control it; the wind is beyond human control.

I would like to suggest another metaphor. When I was growing up, we characterized how things were doing by saying, "That's the way the cookie crumbles." If we do not like the way the cookie is crumbling, we can try to change the recipe. Perhaps that is the way we might look at what is happening in urban transportation.

In many respects the cookie is not crumbling very well, and I think there are ways in which we need to change the recipe. It is not very easy to do: it requires changes in government policy, programs, and regulations. These are the things that we must eventually do, however, if we are to see major improvements in the efficiency of urban transportation.

Financing New Suburban Roads

With regard to the problem of suburban congestion, the headline issue at the moment, there are strong justifications for providing more road capacity in rapidly developing suburban areas. We are far behind in planning and finding ways to finance that expanded capacity, though, and I do not see how the private sector can provide that capacity under the current ground rules. New action on the part of government must be taken. Even the Dulles Toll Road project, which is often considered a harbinger for suburban toll roads, required considerable cooperation among federal, state, and local government agencies, including the provision of the right of way.

A certain amount of private financing of local roads within and adjacent to new developments has always been expected. Limitations on road funds at all governmental levels, however, are currently putting pressure on the private sector to finance much more of the road construction required in conjunction with new land use development. Unfortunately, our present rationale for how this should be done is not very good. It is still quite ad hoc in nature.

The concept of impact fees is receiving a lot of publicity in the Washington, D.C., metropolitan area and in others with rapid suburban growth. Although there is potentially a good economic rationale for this approach, many of the current impact fees seem to be primarily a political accommodation to concerns over rapid growth. Local politicians feel compelled to apply these fees because of pressures from their citizenry about rapid growth and increasing congestion. The larger developments tend to be charged with these fees because they are the visible ones, the ones that make the front page of the newspaper when the local zoning board approves them. Meanwhile, many smaller developments just slip through the zoning approvals one by one without impact fees, even though in aggregate they are creating substantial demands on the road system.

What we need is a more comprehensive way of applying these fees and a better economic rationale or basis for determining them. In most cases, these fees emerge from rather ad hoc negotiations between local government zoning boards and developers. In the long term that is not likely to be a very good basis for financing our road system.

Road user fees are another important issue. As we know, inflation and fuel conservation have eroded the revenues for new roads and road maintenance generated by gasoline taxes. We should certainly ensure that road users cover at least the variable costs occasioned by their use of the road system. This requires more frequent increases in user fees than we have seen, particularly gasoline taxes. Again, this is something the various levels of governments have to work on together.

Some have suggested that we allow privatized roads to use funds from the Highway Trust Fund. Although this is done in Great Britain, I doubt that the political environment in this country would allow it. That is not to say that one could not create some kind of incentive system for faster and cheaper construction of roads. The concept of privatized roads, however, is not likely to be accepted yet.

Toll roads are a fascinating option, not only from the point of view of raising revenue for roads, but also, at some point, for rationing use. As congestion begins to hit the headlines again, we may be able to dust off our old studies of congestion pricing and see if we cannot revive that idea in policy discussion. We have had a successful experiment in Hong Kong with electronic technology to charge for road use at certain congested points. If we are indeed moving toward excessive congestion on major freeways and arterial roads and we cannot expand capacity enough to relieve that congestion, then perhaps we need to start rationing the use of those roads through congestion tolls. If we run out of everything else, that approach is the ultimate remedy.

Traffic Mitigation

Agreements between local developers and local governments to reduce the traffic effects of new developments by implementing ride-sharing programs and minibus services are all encouraging. My concern is that these programs may be limited to small case-by-case improvements that move in the right direction but are insufficient to bring about real improvement on a significant scale. A more comprehensive policy toward road development, land use development, and charges for road use will ultimately be needed.

Transportation Management Associations (TMAs) also fall into the category of encouraging developments. Again, though, if we cannot change the governmental ground rules so these TMAs can be more effective, they will not be able to accomplish very much. Forming a TMA in Tyson's Corner in suburban Virginia, for example, focuses attention on the problem, but it does not provide the leverage to do very much unless government also takes appropriate actions such as providing high-occupancy lanes. TMAs and the business community can do very well in organizing car pooling, van pooling, and minibus services to a major location, like Tyson's Corner, but the difficulty is that they cannot really make the services attractive in terms of reduced travel times by providing exclusive lanes on a piece of roadway. That is what is really needed to make those services viable. Provision of a van, privileged parking, and the like meet only part of the problem.

If local governments became involved in upgrading the arterial roads and providing exclusive lanes in the peak hour for high-occupancy vehicles, those high-occupancy modes would be much more attractive. It is that last ingredient that is still missing.

Providing Suburban Transit

The development of suburban transit systems and the withdrawals of suburban jurisdictions from regional transit services are important trends that are beginning to produce some diversity in transit service, in terms of both vehicle and service types. We have seen cross-suburban minibus routes evolving in place of traditional radial bus services in a number of suburban areas. Unfortunately, though, these systems represent the institution of new public authorities as opposed to opportunities for the private sector. The Montgomery County system in suburban Washington, D.C., is an example. It is much like a publicly owned transit system in a smaller city except that the heavy hand of the federal government is not involved. It does not allow much opportunity for service diversity and has only recently instituted limited competition among providers. That is a worrying aspect about these emerging new suburban systems.

To get the competition and service diversity we need in mass transit, we must make three changes. One is to change local regulations that restrict competition. The second is to change the incentives in our transit assistance programs that tend to encourage capital-intensive, publicly owned systems. And the third is to disburse subsidies competitively rather than distributing them to one organization, whether public or private, without competition.

Some progress has occurred on the third point in a few locations such as Houston, San Diego, and Seattle. Not very much movement has occurred on the other two points, however. Unless we change the structure or the recipe of local regulations and government assistance programs, we face real limits on how far we can move toward more competition.

Financing Transit

Prospects for private financing of mass transit are limited. The winds of change appear to blow only very faintly in this particular area: they can hardly be detected. Again, I think the problems stem primarily from our governmental assistance programs, particularly the federal transit program. Most of the major rail transit investments on the drawing boards are being lined up for federal capital assistance, not for private financing. That is understandable, of course, given the incentives that the federal program presents to local officials.

If we could change the federal role from, for example, providing 75 percent of the capital funds to providing perhaps 25 percent as a match to local funds, private or public, then the winds might blow a little stronger for private financing. Until that situation has changed, however, I do not expect much activity in this area.

I am convinced that the discretionary capital element of the federal transit program is the primary problem there. Even at a reduced funding level, a discretionary capital program leads each city to believe it has a good chance of coming away with a lot of money, if its supporters can just make a strong enough case. Chasing after these discretionary federal funds generally takes precedence over exploring possibilities for private financing.

The interstate road system gave developers a field day to develop around a piece of roadway that they did not contribute a nickel to. People driving their cars and paying their gas taxes into the Highway Trust Fund paid for it. Those taxes built the interstate road system, which provided very great accessibility of land at the interchanges and led to a lot of development.

In a recent article about a new development in Prince George's County, Maryland, the reporter asked the developer, "Why are you coming to Prince George's County when everybody else is going to Fairfax and Montgomery Counties?" The developer replied, "Highway access is the name of the game, and this is where the access is. It's congested in those other counties."

There are still interchanges around the Washington Beltway, in Prince George's County, where the access is very good and the catchment area, as they call it, for cars is very large. We do not have much chance of getting developers to fund mass transit with all that accessibility provided courtesy of the Highway Trust Fund. Perhaps as that runs out, as it is beginning to do, we can get these developers to contribute to some degree, but I expect they will be more interested in roads than in mass transit.

Some have argued that we should give a lot of governmental financial incentives for mass transit. We do already, and I am not sure we want to give any more. Our basic problem is that the transport system is underpriced in general: we need to raise the price, rather than lower it.

I think the concentration of governmental policy initiatives should be on the highways as opposed to mass transit. We should do things that encourage privately operated forms of public transport to

27

expand, like providing exclusive lanes for high-occupancy vehicles. The potential for traditional forms of mass transit, however, given our highway system, is really quite limited, and I doubt that we will see much private financing of mass transit.

In summary, we have seen some very interesting and encouraging private sector developments, and I am sure we would all like to see more of them. I am skeptical, though, that they will expand very much until we change the current recipe of governmental policies and regulations.

5

Private Financing of Mass Transit

Jeffrey A. Parker

Unfortunately, I do not have any case studies of how individuals have surmounted incredible obstacles and confounded conventional wisdom to demonstrate that public transit can actually make money. We are not likely to find many of those examples today.

As public funds for infrastructure investments grow scarce, however, the private sector has come to be viewed as the new wave of capital financing in transit. At the same time, there is considerable confusion over what private participation actually means. I begin by giving specifics about what private financing is not.

What Private Financing Is Not

Private financing, first of all, is not municipal debt. Perhaps here in Washington any funds that are not federal are thought to be private, but elsewhere this is not true.

Bonding nonfederal revenue sources is a legitimate financing tool. It does not constitute private participation in a risk-sharing or economic sense, however. An example often cited in describing private sector financing that is really municipal debt is the issuance of fare box-supported bonds by the New York Metropolitan Transportation Authority (MTA). These bonds are backed by the operating revenues and subsidies received by the New York MTA. Fare revenues account for 54 percent of MTA's operating costs.

How can the MTA issue bonds when it is covering only 54 percent of its costs? The bonds are sustained by trust in the premise that transit service in New York is so vital that fares can be raised to extremely high levels to meet debt service requirements, if other subsidies are cut back.

According to a recent analysis prepared for the governor of New York, however, debt service for the subway system's capital improvement could require $.20 out of the current $1 subway fare by the early 1990s. If only one-half of the capital funds needed for improvements to the New York City Transit Authority beyond 1987 are financed using farebox bonds, the token will have to increase by another $.40 to cover just the additional debt service. By 1993, then, $.60 of the fare will be required just for debt service on farebox-supported bonds if present trends and the interest rates assumed continue.

That is an untenable situation, and it is not a private sector solution to MTA's very real capital needs. Public money capitalized in municipal bond markets is therefore not a private transaction.

The second thing that private financing is not is a tax-shelter deal. Although it is true that Metromedia or GE Credit may own transit assets, safe-harbor transactions merely place public transit agencies in an intermediary role between private taxpayers and the federal Treasury. They are a turnstile, a gatekeeper. No new economic benefits or added value is created for transit by a safe-harbor transaction.

Nonetheless, this is the real world. Transit needs all the support it can muster. The 3 percent reduction in the cost of assets often realized from the sale of safe-harbor assets is a real help, and I think it can be supportive. Let's not call it private sector participation, however.

Similarly, many of the "innovations" in recent transit finance are really complex arrangements designed to exploit nuances in the tax code. For example, the models constructed to realize the goal of building private transit systems in Orlando and to Dulles Airport have hinged largely on structuring huge leases financed at tax-exempt borrowing rates but still preserving accelerated depreciation and investment tax credit benefits. These tax and borrowing schemes have little to do with value. I question basing multimillion-dollar decisions on such modern day alchemy.

On the positive side, both the Dulles and the Orlando examples link transit improvement to significant new land development opportunities, where the real value creation can result from transit investment.

Still another set of so-called private sector transactions involves tax advantages that are aimed at benefiting from arbitrage earnings: that is, borrowing at a low tax-exempt rate and reinvesting at a higher taxable rate. This school of thought runs completely counter to IRS regulations and is really responsible for many of the limitations placed on industrial development bonds over the years.

Efforts to preserve tax breaks for the transit industry are genuine and should receive positive consideration. Their application, however, should be limited to instances where other federal funds or subsidies are not involved.

The kind of financial transaction that I see as being real private sector participation is one where new economic benefits from investment are created and shared: impact fees, special assessments, negotiated investments, joint development, transfers of development rights, and density bonuses are all examples of this kind of mechanism. So, too, are economic leases that reflect actual depreciation and allow transit systems to provide service without owning assets.

There is no question that these, too, may be imperfect tools in their own way. There is, though, a fundamental link between value creation and cost recovery and capital formation.

The Cost of Transit Systems

Thus far, my discussion of private financing has focused on the revenue side of the transit investment issue: where to get the money to pay for rehabilitation and for building new systems. Now we address what I consider the essence of the issue, the tremendous cost of these systems. The cost of building them is tremendous; the cost of maintaining them is tremendous. And our approach to defining capital needs reinforces the whole arrangement.

Although I don't want to be cynical, I think the problem arises because feasibility studies are done by engineers instead of by economists, finance specialists, and developers. What is worse, the engineers' clients are politicians. They are not hard-headed managers who have to control costs and achieve return on investment objectives, or go bankrupt. Engineers want to build, and they are not particular about where the project is or how much it costs. For the price of a feasibility study, a person can acquire an ally to promote his favorite project. Unlike financial analysts, engineers will emphasize physical feasibility first and economics last, if ever. Previously, the feasibility studies and alternative analysis included a section on financing that was similar to the Catalog of Domestic Federal Assistance. The lure of easy money, combined with the spirit to get things done, created an irresistible force.

With the help of engineers, a new demonstration project could always be conceived. Now engineers have caught up to privatization and the tax-motivated transaction. These "innovative approaches" constitute the financing portions of new feasibility studies. Even though they are subject areas that engineers and political scientists know little about, the work seems to suggest that someone will think of the answers once the project is in final design.

The desire for the project still drives the economics, not vice versa. My job as a financial analyst in this backward world is to be clever and to work out how to pay for someone else's grand vision, whether or not it is economically viable. The private sector, however,

31

cannot fulfill that role any more than the Urban Mass Transportation Administration (UMTA) or any other federal agency can.

Beyond economic fundamentals, once the idea of these projects takes root, costs assume a life of their own. Engineers, like all of us consultants, want to please their clients. Certain problems are quite predictable:

• Overbuilding stimulated by available capital dollars (despite the difficulty of finding maintenance dollars in the future) can result in projects with enormous front-end costs.
• Overdesign through preliminary and final engineering is further inflated by inevitable change orders and discrepancies between plans and field conditions.[1]
• Cost problems are multiplied when public procurement procedures and requirements are layered on top of an inherently inefficient process.

The same sorts of inefficiencies that exist among major defense contractors and cause them to operate separate plants for military and commercial production can probably be found among many transit contractors as well. As long as engineers are bent on developing specifications for projects that preclude the use of off-the-shelf products, where are the incentives for contractors to become more efficient?

Every people-mover designed in this country, for example, has had a unique specification attached to it. The bottom line is that unless private participation in transit finance means finding a way to deal with the priority lists for new projects and reining in their cost, no progress will have been made. My job is not to find cash for uneconomic investments, but to help those with financial justification and realistic costs work. Private participation requires sound economic fundamentals.

Benefits of Private Participation in Mass Transit

Having completed the doom-and-gloom portion of my economic message, I now want to become positive and point out some examples of how value and economic benefits can be introduced in the system.

In June 1984, the Port Authority of Allegheny County, Pittsburgh's transit agency, issued over $37 million in thirty-month Advance Construction Notes for completion of a $550 million reconstruction of its light rail system.

During 1983, the agency realized that it could save a substantial amount of money by completing the project faster. Unfortunately, the slow pay out of federal funds did not allow contracts to be let as fast as the Port Authority was ready to build. The notes advanced federal funds due in a future fiscal year under a full-funding contract. In effect, a construction loan was arranged. The result was a $3 million savings in project costs. Yes, this was a tax-exempt financing. Yes, there were some arbitrage benefits. But there was a tangible economic benefit to all parties, a reduction in net project cost.

In a second example, I am managing partner of a venture that is developing a 1.0 million-square-foot office complex in the parking lot at Three Rivers Stadium in Pittsburgh. The project provides for a Westinghouse people-mover system that could connect our project to the Port Authority's light rail transit system in downtown.

Our venture would participate in the financing of this system through a direct capital contribution for our land. In addition, we would underwrite a substantial part of the operating costs and build and operate the entire system on a turnkey basis. The operating costs would be financed from our payments, parking revenues at Three Rivers Stadium, and advertising. We would charge no fares.

What we have learned is this: (1) our capital costs are probably 30 to 50 percent below public construction costs; (2) our operating costs are less than half of a public agency's because of the integration of the people-mover into our building's operating system; (3) Westinghouse will relieve us of the risk of cost overruns on the system by guaranteeing completion at a firm fixed price, partly because we are buying an off-the-shelf system. We have agreed to accept an existing design, thus side-stepping new engineering and product development; (4) we can save a tremendous amount of time and energy by putting a preliminary design out for a design-build competition, something that public procurement simply does not permit; (5) the design-build approach insulates us as developers from cost overruns on the civil portion of the project, which represents two-thirds of the cost; (6) through aggressive management, I believe our operation could have a positive cash flow over time even though we are charging no fares; and (7) we can predict and control maintenance costs through a twenty-year, fixed-price maintenance contract with Westinghouse.

Some will ask how a positive cash flow can be achieved without fares. The additional parking revenues attributable to the project, combined with advertising and incentive fee payments, could allow us to enter into a cost-sharing arrangement with the city, where we have an incentive arrangement that excess revenues will be split.

I believe the same benefits can be achieved by public transit agencies as well. Transactions, though, must be structured with economics first and physical feasibility second. The market for transit investment, in my view, lies in similar small-scale additions to the current bus and fixed-guideway transit network.

Hundreds of such small-scale projects are both possible and necessary. Major projects are also needed in some cities. A rational process for selecting them and controlling their costs, however, is necessary.

In both Washington and its suburbs, Metro has opened new corridors for high-density development. A major federal investment has triggered huge, new private investment; now, spinoff projects must be built. If I ride to Alexandria, Virginia, or Rockville, Maryland, from my office in Washington, for example, I need some type of circulator system to get to a meeting or to the shopping center; otherwise, I will drive my car. For those areas to deal successfully with their internal circulation requirements, at some point they will have to provide either a small shuttle bus or some type of fixed-guideway system that will extend access to Metro stops.

Similarly, if Tyson's Corner in the Virginia suburbs becomes saturated with traffic, how can a street-level or elevated circulator system be developed to reduce automobile congestion within the Tyson's business district and allow the pace of development to continue? In this respect, perhaps the example of the Las Colinas project in Dallas, where an entire new city has been proposed, is of some interest. The developers of that project have formed a municipal improvement district to build, in effect, a private internal transit system. Westinghouse was just chosen to build the starter line of that system, a $20 million contract. As part of the covenants governing the sale of each parcel in the Urban Center of Las Colinas, there are requirements to build a section of guideway. As a result, in Las Colinas today, little stubs of guideway are in evidence near many of the buildings.

One problem that calls for more attention is market orientation and differentiation in the transit business. Right now, all transit systems have the same forty-foot bus or the same cramped, heavy-rail vehicle. I think there is a real market for a premium service that guarantees a seat, that guarantees a comfortable seat, and that the public is prepared to pay for. At the same time, as a private developer, we are not necessarily interested in the lowest-cost, bare-bones kind of system. We want something with real appeal; we want something that we know will work, that will not be covered with graffiti, and that will not be a target for crime. Otherwise, the system is a detriment to the development as opposed to an asset. That is why we offered to operate the people mover system ourselves in Pittsburgh, not because we lack confidence in the Port Authority, but because we want to control it, absolutely and completely.

As for service issues, consider that as part of a bus route study, the New York MTA found some routes in Brooklyn that date back to the time when a ferry service ran between Brooklyn and lower Manhattan. Although the ferries were discontinued in the 1930s, the buses are continuing to serve those ferry-landings fifty years later. Interestingly, developers have recently proposed to re-establish the ferry service! Sometimes we get locked into things in the transit industry that are perpetuated over time, causing real problems. I see that lack of market orientation as the heart of these problems.

Help for Existing Transit Systems

So far, I have touched mainly on new construction. What can be done to meet the enormous needs of existing transit systems? I believe public transit industry suppliers can exert great influence on both capital and operating costs if they are allowed to enter the service market aggressively and if they are challenged by competitive pressures in the leasing and financing business.

For example, bus manufacturers now sell their product on a twelve-year cycle. Transit agencies rely on federal funds, not only to acquire buses, but also to replace them after they wear out. The buses are then maintained in a costly public facility by transit agency employees. Under an alternative scenario, the public agency can acquire the use of these very same assets without having to buy or maintain them. For a fee based on hours of service or mileage, the transit agency could contract for the buses through a package arrangement that included maintenance as well as depreciation. This is exactly the way the transit industry has acquired the use of bus tires from Goodyear since 1921—nothing innovative about it. It can be applied to buses, steel wheels on rail cars, or fare-collection equipment. Any subsystem or major system involved in providing transit service can benefit from this approach.

The opportunities for savings can be very significant. They come about when a market for used equipment can be created. Once a market for used equipment exists, buses and other types of transit assets can become leasable commodities. Today, nobody wants a five-year-old transit vehicle because they can buy a new one instead at virtually the same cost.

We must cut the capital costs to acquire buses and garages. Labor costs associated with maintenance can be controlled and reliability increased. Even if a manufacturer takes over an agency's bus garage or a heavy rail maintenance facility and the private firms inherit those labor contracts, at some point private management capabilities are brought to bear, private cost structures are introduced, and changes can be made over time that affect the dynamics within those buildings. And that is where the real savings can occur.

What motivates the shift in priority is not a tax deal, but an opportunity for the manufacturer or some intermediate organization to generate new profits from the finance and service sectors and the possibility that the market for used buses will become larger and more stable as a result of institutional change. By so doing, we are creating a new carrot for industries that are manufacturing primarily to get into the service business and find new ways to make profits.

The economic benefit is more service at less cost to the public. I call this type of private involvement intermediate-stage competition, introducing competition into the process of producing transit services. Contracting bus routes is end-product competition, which has a role in the industry's future. It has limitations, however.

• First, there are fewer opportunities to achieve line-item savings that could allow public transit agencies in the future to become more cost-effective.

• Second, since the bulk of cost savings from contracting bus routes is achieved through lower driver cost, a downstream change in this factor, such as unionization or legislation at the state or local level, could wipe out the principal benefit in most cities.

• Third, end-product competition cannot be applied to existing fixed-guideway systems. Intermediate-stage competition is one of the few models that can be brought to bear in fixed-guideway applications.

• Fourth, the profit incentive is confined to the private provider. In an end-product competitive model, the provider of that service is the one with the profit incentive. In an intermediate-stage competitive model, those profit incentives are disbursed throughout the industry down to the supplier level, and create greater opportunity for cost savings.

Summary

To sum up, not every example of private participation is either economically beneficial or even private in the end. Engineers should not be allowed to determine the economic feasibility of anything. The term "innovative finance" should be confined to new ways of using transit to create value rather than applied to clever devices to exploit or expand idiosyncrasies of the tax code. And, most important, we should think of private participation as a way to cut costs and create new benefits rather than as a means to pay for something the public simply cannot afford.

Note

1. A change order is a deviation from the final design upon which construction or rolling stock bids are based. If the final design is changed after the bid is accepted, the contractor can increase the price to accommodate the new requirement. Sometimes this can produce huge overruns if materials based upon the original design have already been purchased or if part of the project is already completed and has to be modified.

6
Trends in Transit Financing

Jay Rogers

The United States has sponsored two major public transportation initiatives since World War II: (1) the construction of the interstate highway system that began in the 1950s and (2) the establishment or purchase of owned and operated public transportation systems during the past twenty years.

We are in a period of parenthesis. Federal funding for new highway construction and public transportation systems is not growing at the same pace as the transit needs of an increasingly decentralized population. Indeed, the maintenance costs and operating subsidies required by the current systems will rival the amount of federal, state, and local money available to public transit.

Renewed private investment in the deregulated airline and trucking industries has raised hopes that local public transit systems could offer similar incentives to private investors. To date, private investment in local transportation has primarily focused on automotive markets. (Cars, vans, buses, and the like are included under the rubric of autos.)

Direct private investment in public transit is not likely to play a significant role until transit systems make a quantum leap toward melding public transit systems with consumers' preference for private vehicles. There is technology on the horizon that offers such an opportunity, but its development and application are not likely until early in the next century.

Lack of Consensus on Public Transit

The role of private financing evolves slowly in a period of uncertainty. The most prevalent type of private investment in public transit is a qualitative one: private businesses' investment of time and people in the cooperative planning process that local and regional governments are establishing for mass transit.

In addition to involving private enterprise in transit planning, these regional planning bodies provide a forum for developing a coherent policy to deal with one of mass transit's key problems—the continued decentralization of home and work centers.

Decentralization operates on two levels. There is the familiar geographical decentralization resulting from scattered job centers and commuting populations. The other level is one of process and is reminiscent of "Catch-22." For privately financed public transportation to succeed, a variety of private and public stake holders must reach a consensus; however, increasingly decentralized interests of these stakeholders make it difficult to precipitate that consensus.

In the past, the opportunity to obtain extensive federal funding for construction of new public transportation systems was the rallying point for transit coalitions. In the future, diminished federal funding for public transportation and the increasing costs of renovating and maintaining existing systems will drain federal money for new mass transit systems.

Direct private investment in new public transportation systems tends to require a more stringent demonstration of cost effectiveness than federal funding does. At the same time, communities are more insistent that new systems have the flexibility to serve the variety of needs held forth by transit coalitions and that systems not infringe on certain quality-of-life considerations. These are divergent trends.

Two Bellwether Examples

The proposed construction of a new twelve-mile rail commuter system in Orange County, Florida, is a good example of the role private investment could play in mass transit. The French conglomerate Matra proposed to build and operate a high-tech driverless train system between Disney's Epcot Center and the International Drive tourist area. The project was to be financed by private investment, bank loans, and industrial bonds along with federal and state grants. Federal transit officials endorsed the project. To allay concerns at the county level, Matra eventually offered to reduce significantly the operating fee it would charge the county.

So after five years of planning and proposals, why was the project abandoned in 1986? One reason was that Orange County residents were not convinced the system would meet their hometown needs rather than primarily serving those of the burgeoning tourist industry. The system's long-term success was also in question given the county's uncertain commitment to limitations on road improvements, restricted parking, controls on new construction—all necessary to center future growth around the rail system.

A second example is provided by the proposed Los Angeles rail system. Los Angeles is experiencing problems inherent in establishing a rail system that crosses heavily developed areas along a new public transit right of way. This project was initially rated as one of the most cost effective in the country.

The discovery of methane gas deposits has forced planners to reconsider the proposed subway route. This comes at a time when anticipated reductions in federal funding for public transit have brought cost considerations to the forefront.

Proposals were made to use existing rights of way along the Southern Pacific and Santa Fe branch lines rather than relying on subway tunnels. A preliminary feasibility study estimates capital costs for this proposal are less than 10 percent of the original subway proposal. This study underscores the advantage of using an existing transportation right of way to reduce costs. Offsetting that cost advantage is the "accident factor" long-haul commercial rail tracks pose when juxtaposed to public transit systems. Washington, D.C.'s Metrorail is suffering from this problem.

The quality-of-life issue is caught up in a separate proposal to reduce construction costs for the Los Angeles system. Elevated tracks were proposed across parts of the system since such construction is a little more than half the price for underground tunneling. The scenic signature of an elevated structure across the San Fernando Valley was not part of that community's vision of the future. Community participation in the Metrorail coalition forestalled elevated construction along that portion of the system.

These examples underscore an acute problem. There is a practical and aesthetic limit to the amount of land a developed community will devote to transportation systems. Finessing the issue by tunneling is generally too costly.

An Analogy: Can Autos Transport the Way Bits Transmit?

The communications industry faced some of the same conceptual limitations now confronting public transportation. For the communications industry the key problem was a finite frequency spectrum that was used inefficiently. Confounding the problem were underground trunk routes that could not accommodate all the twisted pair transmission wires required by an exponential growth in traffic.

New communication technologies offered the opportunity to leverage the volume of traffic over existing transmission routes. Coaxial cable and fiber optics improved the transmission "surface," and multiplexing allowed more users to efficiently use communication capacity.

In essence, multiplexers took a singular transmission channel and, acting as computerized traffic cops, directed multiple signals down a path where only single use was previously possible. Enter serendipity and the winnowing of communication monopolies, spurring the introduction of these technologies and reduced communication costs.

In a similar vein, automobiles could be more efficiently directed down peak traffic arteries by one central computer rather than by hundreds of different drivers. The technologies to achieve such a transit scenario already exist. Piecemeal, these individual technologies are now entering the market. The future offers the opportunity to have a broad range of traffic technologies work in concert and produce a quantum leap in roadway efficiency.

New Technologies for Enhancing Road Use and Autos

Managing the public transportation network has not been an easy task in light of the consumer's love affair with the automobile. Transportation planners do not necessarily share consumers' preference for cars. In fact, they have been known to compare autos to roaches, characterizing both as possessing noxious attributes and an uncanny ability to multiply and survive.

For their part, consumers are increasingly aware that a private vehicle's perceived advantages (that it can be driven whenever, wherever, and however the driver wants) produce a cruel irony when all that independence converges on a rush-hour bottleneck. But there is relief on the horizon.

New technology already is being used to solve transit problems in the New York metropolitan area. Sensors embedded in the streets feed traffic information to ten computers monitoring the outer boroughs. This information is processed to establish the most advantageous sequence for traffic signals.

A general rule of thumb is that such computerized systems can achieve a 70 percent reduction in the number of stops drivers have to make at intersections. In 1988, the heart of Manhattan will begin to phase in the outer boroughs' system, using five computers to monitor, analyze, and control traffic flow.

The sprawling road network of Los Angeles is using this technology to fine tune the flow of cars onto freeways. With time and experience, the technology will become more sophisticated in acquiring data and interconnecting networks. The overall goal is to keep more cars on the move.

Currently, interaction between cars and computer traffic networks is limited to traffic signals or traffic center bulletins broadcast over the radio. That could change if the specially designated high-occupancy-vehicle lanes of today evolve into the next century's high-technology-vehicle (HTV) guideways.

New technology will allow specially equipped autos and mass transit buses to use designated roadways more efficiently. Computers could take much of the decision making out of driving, allowing drivers to preprogram destination exits. A driver's new role would be to operate as fail-safe in an emergency, but otherwise to enjoy the ride. The vehicle's entry, speed, driving regimen, and exit would be controlled by public transit's central computer.

Perception technologies (for example, television, lasers, and radar) that communicate with advanced computer architectures and then guide autonomous land vehicles are currently being tested. These vehicles are equipped with artificial intelligence systems and enhanced robotics.

The bottom line of this high-tech litany is that technology is at the critical mass necessary to upgrade existing roadways and the cars using them. The result should be a safer and higher rate of use over HTV lanes.

This technology is still in early development and testing. Some of the most significant work is being done on the Defense Advanced Research Projects Agency's autonomous land vehicle, of which Martin Marietta is the prime contractor. This contract will explore both military and nonmilitary applications.

Will private consumers pay a high price for such systems in their cars? The Houston Chamber of Commerce estimates that traffic jams currently cost the average resident $800 a year in time, gasoline, and insurance. HTV cars and roadways offer riders a way to avoid those costs.

By the turn of the century, the cost and benefits of installing HTV in autos and roadways should intersect at a point that will attract the interest of private investors, public policy planners, and, most important, consumers. Some of the first applications of these technologies are now entering the consumer market. One example is a collision warning system for private vehicles; another is a computerized mapping system that monitors and reports the exact location of a driver's car.

In the interim, public transportation is an unlikely candidate for substantial direct private financing. Of course there will be exceptions. Such exceptions seem least likely for fixed mass transit systems, like heavy rail and subway. These systems cannot adapt to changing commuting patterns. In certain situations, more flexible systems such as bus or jitney services can attract private investors.

Private Enterprise as Intermediary Rather Than Investor

Traffic congestion is forcing residents to accept some local taxes and bond initiatives for building new roadways and funding public transit. Localities, however, are increasingly confronting private developers with "up-front" charges for transit services required by new construction. This puts the private developer in the role of the intermediary who passes these charges on to the buyer or tenant.

Nationwide, localities are implementing innovative programs. Prince George's County, Maryland, for example, has established tax increment financing districts to collect revenues from commercial enterprise. The money goes toward improving transportation. Special benefit assessment districts are another way local governments can recapture some of the economic benefits from transportation improvements.

New developers whose projects will make additional demands on the transportation systems are being required to file impact statements and to pay for public transportation improvements as part of the approval process. In other cases private developers will underwrite their own jitney or people-mover connections to public mass transit systems and pass on the break-even cost as part of the tenant's overhead.

Employers, too, make an indirect contribution to public transportation by permitting flex-time schedules so workers avoid traffic congestion. Van pools are another incremental transit benefit that employers underwrite. Employers will continue to offer employees transit assistance as a way to enhance recruiting from the shrinking labor pool.

Another important way private enterprise plays an intermediary role in public transit is to participate in transit service contracts. Public transit systems are finding such contracts more cost effective than performing the services in-house.

Conclusion

Decentralization, problematic federal funding, and the deterioration of existing systems all present challenges for public transit. Consumers' preference for automobiles is an underlying, but not insurmountable, obstacle. Given this preference, private investors have favored the automobile industry over public transit. But as public transit achieves a better integration of auto, driver, and transit system, private investment becomes more accessible.

An alternative is for consumers to significantly reduce their preference for automobiles. In the near term, traffic congestion threatens to accomplish such an estrangement. New technologies and a resilient consumer demand for automobiles, however, are likely to win out. The result should be a new hybrid of automobiles and public transit.

Part Four

Competitive Contracting:
Some Costs and Benefits

7

Contracting for Transit Service

Roger F. Teal

I would like to give an overview of what we at the University of California, Irvine, have learned over the past three or four years about transit service contracting. In our studies we have looked at the taxicab industry as a source of local demand-response services, at the charter bus industry and school bus carriers as sources of commuter bus services, and at contracting in California; most recently, we have undertaken a national survey of public agencies that sponsor transit to see how much service contracting is taking place. We have also been studying the cost savings of contracting for the Urban Mass Transportation Administration (UMTA).

Service contracting for transit service is by no means a novelty; it is a well established practice. Thirty-five percent of all the public agencies that we surveyed in the country, which included virtually every public agency that sponsors some kind of transit service for the general public, contract for some or all of their service. Yet at the same time, contracted services constitute only about 5 percent of operating expenditures for bus transit and demand-response transit. Thus there is a huge disparity between the amount of money we spend for contract services and the number of services or systems in existence. The primary reason for that disparity is that these services are typically small in scope, usually operating with twenty-five or fewer vehicles. The typical contracted system has less than $1 million in its budget—often less than $200,000.

On the one hand, then, contracting is no novelty; on the other hand, the agencies that would save the most money by contracting—the medium-sized to large transit agencies—are precisely those that do it the least. For example, less than 9 percent of the systems with fifty or more vehicles contract for all of their service. Conversely, twenty-eight percent of the systems with fewer than fifty vehicles contract for all of their service. In other words, among small transit systems, a substantial portion contract out their entire service.

Among big systems—and fifty vehicles is hardly a big system—a tiny portion contract out all their service.

These larger systems, when they do contract, almost always contract out only a small portion of the system, usually a demand-response transit service for the elderly and handicapped. So although there is an enormous market potential for service contracting among medium-sized to large transit organizations, the number of large transit services that are currently contracted out can be counted on the fingers of two hands.

Why Choose Contracting?

Many people have the idea that where service contracting does occur, it is limited to a demand-response system such as dial-a-ride for the elderly and handicapped. That is only partially correct. Contracting is most prevalent for demand-response transit (DRT) services, but 150 fixed-route services are also contracted. This is over 20 percent of all fixed-route systems nationwide.

Most contracting is for municipally provided transit services, over one-quarter of which are contracted out. Over 30 percent of the miles of municipally sponsored services are contracted out. On both a mileage and an operating expenditure basis, municipalities engage in more service contracting than do their counterparts in transit agencies. I believe incentive systems are the reason for this. Municipalities that sponsor transit services often do so with a severely constrained funding base. In many cases they do not have access to federal funds; or if they do, it is a small amount of federal funds. They usually have to use local, general-purpose revenues to support the local subsidy share of their transit service. They do not use dedicated sources from property taxes or sales taxes, as has become increasingly common for medium-sized to large transit systems.

In California, where much of this contracting takes place, money comes from the state. Municipalities not in one of the large urban counties in California can use that money for highway purposes as well as for transit purposes once their "unmet transit needs" have been met in some reasonable fashion. So municipal governments have tremendous incentives to engage in the most cost-effective form of service delivery. Not surprisingly, a substantial number of municipalities have turned to contracting because they have taken the trouble to compare the cost. Or maybe they did not take the trouble to compare the cost, but knew from their experience with other public services that it would cost them more to operate the service in house than to contract it out.

In addition, they believe they might be stuck with the service forever if they operate it in house, no matter what happened to external subsidy sources. This surprising point has come across to me in numerous interviews around the state of California. People in local government wonder what will happen if the state decides to discontinue subsidizing transportation costs. Because the citizens have come to depend on the transportation service, they will not be willing to give it up. But if a public bureaucracy operates the service, the costs of operation will probably be high (as with large transit agencies), which is precisely what they want to avoid.

It is also interesting to note that contracting is concentrated in a relatively small number of states. California, Massachusetts, Minnesota, and New York are among the states where contracting is particularly prevalent.

Again, if you look at the incentive structure in those states, the logic of this pattern becomes clear. In Minnesota, Massachusetts, and New York state money goes to the localities after it has been appropriated by the state legislatures. In New York, the appropriation is calculated in part according to the number of vehicle miles traveled. Accordingly, the localities have an incentive to get the most vehicle miles per dollar.

In the municipalities where the money comes down from the state, therefore, there is a strong incentive to use it in the most cost-effective fashion. Not surprisingly, those are the places where contracting is most prevalent.

These experiences suggest that when the incentive structure itself encourages the cost-effective use of subsidy dollars, contracting occurs by itself, and it is not really necessary to mandate targets. California contracts out over two hundred public transit services to the private sector. There is no specific state policy in California to promote private sector contracting. It has just happened as a natural result of the incentives built into the state's transit subsidy program.

I think it is also instructive that contracting in California has not happened in the large urban transit districts where the money goes only to transit. When funds come just to transit agencies and cannot be used for highways or other transportation purposes, little contracting occurs.

Characteristics of Service Contracting

Our nationwide survey has given us an understanding of the nature of service contracting today. One of the objectives of the survey was to determine how such things as competition, length of contracts, vehicle ownership, etc., affected the contracting decision.

Length of Contracts. We found that most contracts are of relatively short duration, one to two years. There are, however, some instances of agencies getting tied into long-term contracts. Massachusetts, for example, has a lot of contracted services. Upon closer examination, almost all are examples of private sector operation of a service that has been pulled into the public sector in every way but ownership. Private monopolies continue to operate; or the same two or three companies control the service. Thus, particularly in the East, some of the old franchise arrangements are still in effect.

In most of the rest of the country, however, contract lengths are consistent with competitive contracting. Contracts are made for relatively short periods. For fixed-route service, the length of contract seems to be related to the issue of vehicle ownership. The length of fixed-route contracts averaged two to four years, with the longer contracts used primarily when the contractor provides the vehicles.

We found that competitive contracting per se is used only 50 percent of the time, but this is not really an accurate reflection of the competitive situation. If one eliminates contract renewals—which typically would be used by an agency that was satisfied with the performance of its contractor—from the calculation, about 70 percent of all contracts are competitive. We believe this figure to be a more accurate reflection of the level of competition.

Vehicle Ownership. Relative to the issue of vehicle ownership, we found that about 50 percent of the vehicles were owned by the private operators, primarily those providing demand-response services. Of the fixed-route vehicles, about 80 percent are owned by the sponsors. This indicates that the sponsors either have access to capital subsidies or would like to keep their costs relatively low by acquiring the vehicles themselves and not having to pay risk premiums to the operators. Risk premiums are charged by contractors that provide their own vehicles, as they must make some allowance for a loss on disposal of the vehicles if the contract is not renewed. Agencies thus seem to make an economic decision, namely to provide the vehicles themselves if they are expensive, or to be more willing to ask the operator to provide them if they are cheap.

The only exception is commuter services, which use the vehicles for only a few hours a day. There the preference is to have the operator provide the vehicle. It makes a great deal of sense for the operator to provide over-the-road coaches that can be used in charter service, since they can use the same vehicle in other services and keep the depreciation relatively low for the contract operation.

The Magnitude of Service Contracting. The total cost of contracted services is a small fraction of the service costs of the typical public agency. The average contracted service costs less than a million dollars, and the median price is less than $200,000. The "typical" contracted service, therefore, is relatively small and inexpensive. Although 35 percent of transit services are contracted, contracted services constitute only 5 percent of the total national expenditures on transit, and about 8½ percent of the total transit miles.

Does Contracting Save Money?

Our studies bear directly on the issue of the cost impacts of contracting. We have looked at this issue in four different ways. First, our national survey gathered information on costs for both public and private operators. It is hard to know how good the information is, but because it is averaged across a relatively large number of systems the chance of large errors is relatively low.

We found the following: For small services, contracting provides little overt cost savings. I say little overt cost savings because we compared actual private systems with actual public systems. Presumably, the small local governments that have chosen to contract calculated in advance that their costs would be lower by contracting than by operating the service themselves. Obviously, those services that *might* have been provided in the public sector could have been more expensive than existing public agency services, but no data exist to prove that. So if the data indicate a 5 to 10 percent saving for small services, it's not necessarily indicative of what the actual range of saving might be in a particular circumstance. Nonetheless, the point is that cost savings from contracting for small systems will be limited, largely because the alternative, operation by a relatively small municipal government, tends to be relatively low cost.

It is the larger systems that save the most by contracting. Because the sample size is quite small for the larger systems, it is hard to extrapolate directly from the data that we have gathered, but we found a 25 to 40 percent cost difference for the larger systems, depending on the size of the private operators whose costs were compared.

We also looked at the potential cost savings from contracting a portion of a large system to a medium-sized privately contracted operation. Typically, a medium-sized to large transit agency would not contract out all of its services. It will contract out pieces of the

51

operation, 15, 25 vehicles, or even 50 to 100 vehicles, but not the entire system. In this situation, the data indicate that the costs would be 30 to 50 percent less for the private operator.

Second, in a separate survey we asked public agencies engaged in competitive contracting for fixed-route service to estimate what their costs would have been if they had chosen to have the service operated by a public agency, either by themselves or by the public operator in their jurisdiction.

It is hard to say how meaningful these estimates are, as they are based on a hypothetical situation. Nonetheless, the estimated cost savings averaged about 30 percent, although their estimates ranged from 0 percent to 50 percent. Obviously, most agencies think they are saving substantially by contracting.

Third, we developed cost models for public agency services and cost models for private operator services. Those cost models were based on actual costs of public agencies and private operators.

We used the concept of avoidable costs; that is, what costs would the public agency avoid by not providing a particular service itself and by contracting for it through private operators. In calculating avoidable cost one cannot eliminate all administrative costs; agencies still have to plan, carry on marketing activities, and provide customer information; facilities still require maintenance. Since administrative costs consume about 15 percent of a typical transit agency's operating budget, and many cannot be avoided when one contracts, a decision to contract out 10 percent of service probably will result in a cost reduction of less than 10 percent.

We also looked very carefully at labor costs and went into great detail in estimating the avoidable labor cost for drivers.

We have tested the model we developed on four large systems of 200 to 800 vehicles, on three small systems, and on another system of about 150 vehicles. The results were as follows.

The estimated savings for large systems were 12 to 39 percent. The largest saving, 39 percent, was for the biggest system, which also had the highest peak to base ratio. They were paying an enormous amount of money for service that they were providing only during the peak period. This was due to high driver costs, which had to do with their driver scheduling needs. The agency with 200 vehicles saved 12 percent. It had a lower ratio of peak to base costs and lower overall costs. The medium-sized system, with 150 vehicles, saved about 15 percent. For the small systems, we found savings ranging from 0 percent to about 12 percent.

These results are based on detailed cost models. We have a great deal of confidence in the public agency cost models. We have less confidence in the private operator cost models, but their results are quite plausible.

Finally, some of the most powerful evidence of cost saving comes from the small number of cases of direct substitution of a privately contracted service for a publicly operated service. There are very few of these around because of the constraints having to do with labor contracts and section 13c of the Urban Mass Transportation Act.

Yolo County, California, previously contracted for service with the Sacramento Regional Transit Authority and then switched to contracting with private operators. The result was a 37 percent cost saving. This is not something that we computed with a model. Yolo County spent X number of dollars one year, Y number of dollars the next year, and X minus Y was several hundred thousand dollars— money in the bank.

Norfolk, Virginia, converted outlying fixed-route services into zoned demand-response services. Our calculation of the cost saving was about 44 percent. This estimate is somewhat problematic because we had to use their cost allocation model; obviously, that could over-estimate what their costs of that service were. Nonetheless, a 30 to 40 percent cost savings would certainly be indicated.

When Carson, California, solicited bids for its services, the low bid from a private operator was more than 50 percent less than the next lowest bid from a public agency.

These few examples lend support to the conclusion from the other studies that cost savings in the range of 30 to 50 percent are achievable, particularly for large transit agencies.

Administrative Issues

Contract management is an important issue that is often raised as an obstacle to contracting by those who have other reasons for not wanting to get into contracting. Our surveys, however, revealed very few problems with contract management. It does not cost a lot of money—typically 3–5 percent. The cost, of course, does depend on the scale of the system. For a small system with only a $300,000 budget, contract management may cost 10 percent, but for a million dollar system, the cost is usually about 5 percent.

We found that the people doing contract management in organizations that do a lot of contracting were very creative individuals. They knew what they were doing. They worked well with their contractors. There was a typical amount of grumbling about the contractor, but there were no serious problems that could not be worked out.

Some agencies that were resistant to the notion of contracting have dramatically turned around. The bureaucracy of the Orange County Transit District initially was skeptical about contracting, but they have become quite enthusiastic about it as it has saved them money and as they have learned how to work with private operators. Similarly, the Houston transit agency has seemed to become more accepting of contracting over time.

Large transit agencies often have highly structured contract management systems. Smaller ones may have less formal systems. We have found that people adapt their systems to fit their circumstances.

Unfortunately, we do not have much experience with large contract operations. The Dallas regional transit authority has probably the most interesting example of a large competitively contracted operation for regular fixed-route service. It will be very interesting to see how that experience works out.

Obstacles to Contracting

I will conclude with a few remarks about what seem to be the key obstacles to contracting. As we talked to people around the country, certain major obstacles were mentioned over and over. One is the incentive system for transit fiscal decisions. Because transit agencies have no incentive to minimize subsidies, they do not always seek to institute the most cost-effective operating methods. That is a major problem. If an agency does not have the flexibility to use its funds for other local government services or for other transportation services, it will not have the incentive to maximize cost effectiveness in transit.

The second obstacle is transit labor. Transit labor is adamantly opposed to service contracting because of the likely effect on union membership and the likely long-run implications for wages and work rules.

The obstacles from the transit industry, however, are not rooted only in transit labor. The third major obstacle is transit management. Transit managers are either overt or in many cases closet opponents of contracting. They have become used to having control of all aspects of service provision and are often hostile to the concept of service contracting. Given the central role of transit management in the decision-making structure at the local level, it is obvious that a relatively long-term process is going to be required to introduce service contracting on a significant scale.

That is perhaps a sobering conclusion, but I do not see quick fixes with service contracting. Municipalities with an incentive system already in place have implemented service contracting. The locations without an incentive system to maximize contracting have been operating in the public monopoly mentality for a long, long time and are resistant to change. Inducing them to change through the non-hierarchical government structure we have in this country is going to be a long, difficult process.

8

Competitive Contracting and the Strategic Prospects of Transit

Wendell Cox

I became interested in the concept of involving the private sector in public transportation four years before the Urban Mass Transportation Administration (UMTA) published its policy. At that time people viewed my ideas with incredulity because they seemed so farfetched. Time has borne me out, however, and over the years I have accumulated a lot of experience in this area and have contributed to the development of the philosophical basis underlying the concept of privatization in the transit industry.

Today's Strategic Situation

Let us first consider the strategic situation of transit at the moment: where we are going, what the choices are that face us, and how those factors relate to competitive contracting, the element of privatization that is especially relevant to transit today. The past being prologue to the present, we need some review of where we have been in public transit to gauge where we are going. The fact is that transit in this nation is faced with a very serious cost crisis—not a *funding* crisis, a *cost* crisis.

Since 1970, real costs of transit operation—that is, cost per mile—have risen by 52 percent. After adjustment for inflation, then, it costs more than three dollars today to buy what we bought in 1970 for two dollars. Out of the $10 billion that we as a nation are paying for public transit this year, nearly $4 billion represents cost increases in excess of inflation. In 1983, 65 percent of the operating subsidies were committed to cost increases above the inflation rate that have occurred since 1970. Only about 35 percent of the money that we have committed to operating subsidies in transit, then, has gone to lower fares or increased services—only 35 percent has resulted in public benefit.

Therefore, when people ask what we will do with the extra

money if costs decline, as a former local transit official, I can assure them that our present transit needs are more than enough to absorb the hypothetical "extra" funds. There will never be enough funds. One of our real problems is that we in transit have lost a great opportunity as a result of our failure to extract value for the subsidies already given to public transit.

The inflation in public transit costs has been so severe that it has even surpassed the increase in medical care costs. Since 1970 public transit costs have increased 37 percent more than medical care costs in this country. In my view, that means a cost crisis, not a funding crisis.

While we are perhaps justified in criticizing the industry for its performance, I do not believe that the industry could have done much to make it any better. What is important now is to look toward the future.

A regression analysis of the years 1970 through 1983 of the annual cost increases of transit suggests elements in a grim scenario for the year 2000: with no changes in present operations real costs in transit will increase by at least another 37 percent, and to continue financing today's level of service and today's real fare levels, we will need $18 billion of new revenue between now and then. I see every reason to trust this prediction.

How might we finance such a thing? One way would be to increase fares and cut services. What degree of fare increases and service cuts would it require to finance expected transit performance over the next fourteen years?

After permitting inflationary fare increases, we would still need an additional 160 percent real increase in fares, if we assume that half of the increase has to be financed by fares. We can further anticipate that we will need to see transit service decline at least 15 percent to pay for the other half of this unfunded deficit.

Another way of achieving it is to provide an increase in public funding support of about 50 percent. Analysts do not anticipate new public funding for transit, however. As I travel through the country, I see few areas eager to pass new transit taxes to pay for yesterday's service levels. As a result, I see a very serious crisis in our future; if we fail to begin dealing with it now, we may very well find ourselves with very seriously constrained urban mobility. The year 2000 may make 1986 look favorable by comparison.

Some transit officials suggest that it is unfair to compare the rise in transit costs to the inflation rate, because somehow transit is a bit different. The American Public Transit Association (APTA) has proposed an index to gauge the increases in transit costs.

I see three good reasons for rejecting this view and the circular

APTA index, however. First, the incomes of the riders are not even keeping up with inflation. Therefore, we must control the rise in transit costs to eliminate the gap between fare increases and transit cost increases, or mobility will decline for these people.

Second, the incomes of the taxpayers who pay most of the costs of operating the systems are also rising, at best, with the consumer price index. They will not be willing to subsidize public transport at levels so far above the inflation rate. These, then, are two political reasons.

But a third, more practical reason is that costs in transit can be kept within the inflation rate, as the private bus industry has proved beyond the shadow of a doubt. From 1970 to 1983, per-mile costs in the private bus industry increased at a rate 3 percent below the inflation rate. At the same time that transit costs were going up a real 60 percent, then, private costs were going down a real 3 percent, in effect creating a 39 percent relative decline in private transit costs during those same years.

Why is it that transit costs are out of control? As I see it, the present structure guarantees that costs will spin out of control. I am convinced that transit management has not failed—I am convinced that transit management could not conceivably have succeeded in the present environment. Not even Lee Iacocca himself could have made a substantial difference.

Transit's structure is fatally flawed. For years on the Transportation Commission and in my experience since that time, I have heard excuse after excuse about why we cannot control these costs. In the middle 1970s, for example, when we hoped to control transit costs by improved performance measures, we bought new computers; we did not improve transit performance. Then we planned to improve transit performance by using part-time labor—since then analysts have shown convincingly that part-time labor had no real overall impact upon transit costs. Yes, indeed, it lowers the cost of peak-hour service, at the same time that costs of other services rose at a more than compensating rate.

Finally, a story from Los Angeles illustrates the situation well. Three years ago, we were conducting a state-mandated performance audit of the Southern California Rapid Transit District (RTD). The consultants reported that the RTD had a very serious absenteeism problem costing the system about $20 million per year. We called in the top RTD management, who assured us that although they had had a problem, they had solved it by putting in some management systems. It is not surprising to me that the latest performance audit now under way has uncovered virtually the same deficiency—indeed nothing has improved. It is not that the RTD management failed to take absenteeism seriously: the problem is that transit has no competitive incentives; there is nothing to induce the right kind of cost performance.

The same forces operate at the policy level: the incentives are all wrong. The problem in transit is that it is a local service monopoly with no incentive to control costs. Frankly, short of injecting competition into the system, we have virtually no hope of controlling these costs.

As a result, I predict a very difficult future for transit without some substantial changes. We must recognize that tinkering with the present organization will not accomplish what is needed.

Competitive Financing

Let us consider the alternative of competitive contracting. Some think of competitive contracting as franchised contracting or contracting with existing operators—not so. A competitive contracting arrangement is one in which all potential operators, including the public operator, offer their bids as equals.

What does competitive contracting do? Simply stated, government buys services from the private sector. As the Citizens League of Minneapolis–St. Paul put it, "The essential function of government is deciding. Government may later itself do what it has decided should be done, but equally it may not. Its basic intention is to ensure that what it has decided should be done is in fact done." Accordingly, a multitude of municipal and county governments around the country have begun to contract or have even already contracted a number of services competitively, including the school bus service (27 percent) nationwide and services like garbage collection. The U.S. Postal Service moves its mail on the ground between major cities 100 percent by competitive contracting. And there are many other examples.

As applied to transit, under a competitive contract arrangement the authority or municipality in charge would continue to set the fares, establish routes, and decide which, if any, routes should be contracted out. Indeed, as is being done in San Diego County, California, and in Seattle and elsewhere, the public agency can specify how the buses are painted so that the system looks like an integrated service.

What would be the impact on labor? This is, obviously, a concern. And if we use the driver attrition rate (about 5 to 7 percent) to bring in contracting, we can largely eliminate the anticipated deficit that I have suggested with respect to the year 2000.

If we use the driver attrition rate of 5 percent and assume cost savings of about 30 percent in the larger and medium systems, we effectively obtain cost control in public transit between now and the year 2000. We can guarantee today's transit employees their jobs but require that in exchange for that security we must have the authority to contract within that attrition rate, so that sufficient cost savings can be achieved to preserve service for the public.

Of course, a private sector is already in place; we do not have to create the entrepreneurial system. There are now some 18 companies nationally that are interested in contracts around the country. The private bus industry is all over the country. There are some 90,000 school buses owned by private operators, not to mention the very large complement of taxi operators. In fact, there are more than four times the number of privately owned buses in this country than are necessary to meet a daily peak requirement in the transit industry. Beyond that, an American Bus Association survey showed that about 90 percent of those operators are interested in buying new equipment if they can obtain contracts for public transit service.

What are the results, then, of competitive contracting in public transit? In Carson, California, for example, the winning private contractor submitted a bid 60 percent lower than the regional transit agencies' operating costs alone.

Snohomish County, Washington, will be saving 38 percent directly as a result of using private contracting for its express system into the city of Seattle.

Cost savings, therefore, are the first reason why competitive contracting makes sense. The second reason is that private costs are lower than public costs, as the experience of the private bus industry illustrates; moreover, a number of studies have shown that private costs rise more slowly than public costs and remain generally within the inflation rate.

A third reason for looking at competitive contracting is that it moderates the increase in public costs. In San Diego and Norfolk public costs of the transit agency have already climbed at a slower rate, and two studies have documented the fact that private costs have created a competition that has begun to affect public costs. This parallels experiences in other disciplines in competitive contracting of public services.

Finally, a very interesting but often ignored consequence is that the public sector can buy better service from the private sector, oftentimes, than it can provide itself with its own resources. Houston, for instance, penalizes its contractors for failing to get air-conditioned buses on the street, for failing to perform on time, and the like. A

good many public transit agencies could not achieve such performance standards—indeed some don't even try to keep the air con-
ditioning working.

An interesting incident occurred in Johnson County, Kansas, a
few months ago when private operators and the potential local public
agency in Kansas City were bidding for service. That local public
agency, as a condition of its bidding for service, sought exemption
from twenty-eight conditions of the contract. The winning private
contractor sought no such exemptions.

What, then, are the factors that will determine success in competitive contracting, that will result in better service to the riders and
better service to the taxpayers funding such systems?

It is critical to have public leadership that is objective, not public
leadership that simply favors the private sector. The private sector is
not seeking unfair advantages; this is not an affirmative action program. This is a program to bring to the public transit industry the
most cost-effective service for both the riders and the taxpayers.

9

Privatization in
the Transit Industry

Philip J. Ringo

I have been in the business of transportation for sixteen years and have been on both sides of the fence on the privatization issue. In the early 1970s, those in the private sector were the whipping boys of the industry. Accordingly, we kept a low profile. During the middle years, the late 1970s, there was so much money spent on transportation that we could go on about our business, and people left us alone.

In the past three or four years, however, the environment has changed again, something I find interesting and amusing. I do not think the private sector was ever as bad as it was portrayed, nor do I think we are ready for sainthood: some balance is necessary.

During those sixteen years, I have also seen fads come and go, and I see a danger in thinking that privatization is just another one. I do not think it is, and I will cite some examples of things going on in the field to illustrate my point. Many will be surprised at new trends in this area and at how privatization really can work and is in fact working.

First, privatization will not work simply because I or anyone else wants it to; it will not work through the power of wishful thinking. It will work because it makes economic sense in the context of public policy. In the transit industry if private sector activities work, they work because they strike a balance between the policy and the political needs of the public sector—and those needs are real. Perhaps we wish they were not there, or would wish them away, but they are real. There is a public sector responsibility when transit service is placed on the street. And I respect that.

On the other hand, to get value out of the private sector, we have to allow the private sector to do what it does well: take risks, to make a profit. A balance must be struck, and if we can accomplish that, we can make real progress.

Collectively, I believe we can reduce costs, maintain or even improve quality of service, and make a profit. When that happens, the taxpayer benefits, the private sector benefits, and the user benefits: a neat win-win-win situation. Perhaps that sounds trite, but that is the way I see it.

The Present State of Privatization

Some interesting things are happening in public transport. First, the private sector marketplace is clearly growing. To cite our company's experience, three years ago we were doing contract management, one aspect of the private sector in competition. We had no turnkey contracts, however, so that type of work accounted for none of our business. Now it is 50 percent and growing at the rate of about 25 percent a year. We see turnkey contracts as ultimately providing 75 percent of our business, with a compound growth rate of at least 20 percent. From our standpoint, this is a real growth market.

Some have estimated the current market for private sector activities at around 5 percent. Some of that market is illusory, of course, and is more franchise contracting than a real, competitive private sector activity. I think the real market is actually about 2½ to 3 percent.

We believe that percentage will grow to 20 percent over the next four to five years, and we are counting on that. If so, that will be a $2 billion market, a size that will surely attract some attention, as indeed it already has. I believe that the market is growing, and that that growth has been demonstrated.

What is happening is competition. Where there is a lot of money, people are eager to compete for it. The example of Snohomish, Washington, is a good case study. Community Transit in Snohomish wished to contract for operation of nine commuter express routes focused on downtown Seattle. In Snohomish four national firms bid on the contract: Trailways, Laidlaw, Bus Lease, and my company; Seattle Metro, the public provider, also bid. Four fairly substantial firms—and I flatter ourselves to put us in that company. It was an interesting and very strongly competitive process, which, by the way, we won. The operating cost we bid was approximately one-half that of the public service provider.

The same thing is happening right now in a competition for transportation services to the Saturn plant in Tennessee. Again, it is a major competition with many people putting a lot of time and money into it.

Coalitions are beginning to form in the marketplace, where companies with major resources are seeking out firms like ours. For example, we are in discussions to be acquired by Ryder Systems. Big companies see this market and believe that it is changing. The projected $2 billion to $3 billion market is the impetus behind those new coalitions, and the degree of investment in their activities is evidence of faith in the future of the market.

New Attitudes across the Board

Moreover, suppliers and manufacturers are taking new attitudes toward risk. Frankly, for many years, we never really explored competitive possibilities with bus manufacturers. We relied on the bid process. That is changing radically, however. Bus manufacturers are now approaching us with ideas on how to put bids together, agreeing to take residual risk with us, and creating an aftermarket for the buses. These things have never happened before in my twenty years' experience in this business. The willingness of suppliers to take risks reflects a changing marketplace.

This new attitude occurs across the board with a wide range of manufacturers, not just with General Motors. People look at the marketplace, see a value, and want to share the risks.

Indeed, surprising as it may sound, I sense new approaches and attitudes on the part of labor. I view the notion that the private sector works only if there are no unions involved as a myth. I do not believe it. We run eighteen turnkey operations in California, where 40 percent of the employees are Teamsters.

Accordingly, I do not think that the situation with unions and unionized employees is the barrier that it is made out to be, nor do I think that private sector operation is, per se, nonunion. I say that advisedly and carefully, but I really believe it. I believe that Section 13c, although a difficult situation, can be dealt with, through attrition perhaps, as well as, in practical terms, through the realization that acknowledging the rights of labor employees does not preclude the possibility of successful negotiation. Union labor is not intractable.

Operating innovations are being implemented; more flexible bidding processes are coming to pass. In Snohomish, for example, we were able to take the specifications and suggest better bus routes, thereby saving the county about $600,000 in capital costs through something no one had seen before. The county authorities were smart enough to approve the changes. We are not geniuses, of course, but we saw something they did not see. And the procurement process was flexible enough to allow that kind of thing to happen.

Other examples come to mind. One of my competitors has a big contract in the southwest, where he is doing some very clever things through increased use of his equipment: he is running charters up to Indian reservation bingo games, taking equipment that is not in use on the weekends. I commend him for it.

I see better use of existing facilities. We are joining with Ryder Systems and GM in other situations. In some cases, where they have underused facilities in place, they are finding ways to use the facility. Again, this represents a practical and economic approach to doing business. True cost savings are being generated.

Why has my company been able to save money? We are running with lower overheads, we are generating lower fringe costs, and in some cases we use lower and, we think, more market-oriented wage rates. If a good driver can be hired for $7.50 per hour, it makes no sense to pay $12.

Moreover, lower rates can be achieved with comparable quality. If they cannot, then the contract will be lost. Cost savings do exist, however. What is the contradiction? Every situation will not yield 30, 40, or 50 percent savings, as the growing myth would have it. Some circumstances may make such savings possible, but in many cases, savings are in the single digits—even 5 percent is worthwhile. It is important to put savings in perspective; they do exist, but must be evaluated correctly.

I also strongly believe that attitudes are changing, even the attitudes of transit managers and the transit industry. It is true that transit managers have resisted changes and that they will continue to do so in some cases. I have seen those attitudes starting to change, however, even with American Public Transit Association. APTA has formed a task force on privatization, and those people are smart transit managers, they are listening, and they will respond, not for any reason other than the fact that the economics are convincing.

Some of the things that the Urban Mass Transit Administration (UMTA) is doing, especially allowing capitalized leases to be paid for through capital dollars, take away a huge barrier to competition. If that obstacle is removed, we are playing on an even field.

People are also starting to become enthusiastic about transit as a career again. More people who come into this business see a future there. Frankly, for a couple of years, in the late 1970s and early 1980s, good people were leaving this industry. That trend appears to be slowing down now. We are starting to recruit at colleges again and to do the things that signify a healthy business.

Will we get the entrepreneurs? Will we be able to compete with Morgan Stanley and American Express? No, but we never were, really. Some very good people like working in the public-private sector partnership. They like running things. Indeed, a person can get working experience very quickly in this business, much quicker than in many other operations or industries.

People will work for incentives, and that is the great thing about the private sector. With an incentive-based contract, people can be hired, given a good base salary, and promised a portion of the fee, if the contract is brought in under budget. People accept that challenge. It is a different approach and it is beginning to work.

Some of the myths are being punctured. Some people said, in the past, "Turn the job over to a private operator and the quality is poor and the service bad." But we are getting a track record, and that is what works in the marketplace. It is neither rhetoric nor salesmanship—it is the track record.

Remaining Problems

The present situation is not without problems, though. Let me turn to the negative.

There have been some procurements where bid specifications were so tight and had so many constraints that it was literally impossible to bid, except for one bidder. This happened recently in the southwestern United States. Although no official will admit it, they paid far too much because they were so tight on the procurement specifications, and the client suffered for it.

On the other side, there have also been some failures of privatization projects. Some commercial projects have failed where bids were too low and the contractor defaulted, leaving the public sector to pick up the pieces. The private sector, then, has not been without sin, because there have been some failures. Unfortunately, that kind of thing happens in the market.

In addition, some transit managers and public officials play games. We have a current bid specification with a 300 percent performance bond—that is patently absurd. It was for ten new buses to be run for two hours of service during a one-year contract. No one is going to buy a new bus, amortize it, take the risk that the costs of twenty hours a day over a year can be covered, and agree to a 300 percent performance bond. It is a joke.

Conclusion

Privatization is coming, and it will grow. It will happen quicker, better, and more efficiently, however, if we put it in perspective. Privatization is not a cure-all. It is not for everybody. Although it can save money, it will not always save 30 or 40 percent—10 percent is acceptable to me.

Privatization is not without risk for the private entrepreneur, who puts money on the line. Nor is it without risk to the public sector.

Privatization can work. We need a little less inflammatory rhetoric that privatization is the savior of all time, however. We clearly need less resistance from operators and managers and more sanity in the bid procedure. To borrow a phrase, I see us going into "intermediate stage competition," where the incentives are creating pressures for cost savings. And that, to me, makes a lot of sense. Privatization can work within the context of the public transit framework.

Part Five

American Innovations in
Public Transit

10
Revitalizing Urban Transit
Robert Cervero

Airlines, railroads, trucking, and intercity buses have all been deregulated in recent years, with bipartisan support and generally good
results. Government is getting out of the friendly skies and off the
busy roadways of this nation so that market forces can prevail. But
although the cross-country rider now benefits from lively competition, the cross-town rider unfortunately does not. In most of our big
cities, public transit users must deal with entrenched monopolies
offering unresponsive services at standardized regulated fares. There
is no reason why this should have to be so. Applying the principles of
deregulation to urban settings could help solve some of the worst
transportation problems plaguing our cities.

The Urban Transit Mess

Those problems are all too familiar to most Americans. Traffic jams
are daily rituals in many places. Moreover, roads and bridges are
approaching the end of their design lives and falling apart, in large
part because maintenance and rehabilitation have been routinely de-
ferred. Public transit shares these upkeep and crowding problems.
Several older subways are rapidly decaying, and in most large cities
buses carry crush-loads in the rush hour but run half empty the rest
of the time. Transit has crippling financial problems as well. Few of
our municipal bus systems recoup more than 40 percent of their
operating costs from fares, saddling governments with most of the
bill. Federal, state, and local subsidies to public transit have grown
from $132 million in 1970 (mostly small capital grants) to over $5.0
billion in 1983, a 3,800 percent rise. Meanwhile, federal expenditures
on highways increased only 109 percent, from $4.4 billion to $9.2
billion, with much of the gain eaten up by inflation. This shift in
national policy reflected the view, shared by Republicans and Demo-
crats alike, that public transit was "good for cities."

Despite this massive infusion of government aid, there has been little payoff to brag about. Nationwide, transit ridership has remained fairly stagnant at about 6 billion passengers a year since 1970. By comparison, urban highway travel has risen from 570 billion miles a year to nearly 1 trillion. The availability of subsidy dollars for public transit, many argue, has typically resulted in lax management, overly generous wage settlements, and the unbusinesslike expansion of services into low-density suburban markets. Public transit's outright legal monopoly in some cities, along with the large subsidies it receives, has tended to squelch competition from taxis, private commuter buses, and other alternative services of generally higher quality.

In all likelihood, deregulation would do more to improve the quality of urban transportation and reduce the fiscal shortfall, in both the highway and transit sectors, than any other policy strategy. Perhaps the greatest appeal of deregulation lies in its potential for spawning a richer mix of services. When traveling in cities today, many Americans have at best only two alternatives to the private automobile—buses or taxis. The past decade, however, has taught us that fixed route, uniform-quality services—buses and subways—will not lure significant numbers out of their cars. Studies consistently show that commuters are far more sensitive to the *quality* of transportation than to its *price* and will give up their cars only if they can, say, dramatically reduce travel time or improve comfort. Factors such as door-to-door travel time, reliability of schedules, certainty of getting a seat, and temperature control are important determinants of what modes travelers choose. Travelers particularly hate to spend time walking to a bus stop, waiting, and transferring.

What is needed, then, is a wider assortment of urban transportation services targeted to the needs and travel desires of a fairly diverse urban America. Regulatory reform could bring this about by injecting a much-needed dose of competition into urban transportation, just as it has already done with the nation's airlines, railroads, and roadways.

Deregulating Taxi, Dial-a-Ride, and Jitney Services

The term "paratransit" is used to describe urban transport services that fall between those of the private automobile and the conventional bus. Taxis, dial-a-ride vans, and jitneys, which comprise one class of paratransit services, respond immediately to travel requests made by phone or curbside hail, and for this they charge a premium. By comparison, van pools and commuter buses are prearranged and operate only between given points. Allowing all types of paratransit

72

to operate freely is a necessary first step toward effectively dealing with today's urban transportation problems.

Taxis. All U.S. cities regulate taxis to some degree. While few observers question the propriety of regulating driver "fitness," the same cannot be said for controlling the number of taxis that operate in a city, the types of services they provide, and the rates they charge. Most cities restrict entry by fixing the number of licenses (medallions) granted, often on the basis of cabs per capita, but a handful of cities, notably Los Angeles and Chicago, achieve the same result by granting exclusive franchises to one or a few companies. Because of these restrictive practices, large fleets offering services of fairly uniform quality have become the norm in most big cities. Medallion and franchise cities more often than not have higher fares than cities that allow virtually unrestricted entry into the taxi market. In Washington, D.C., an unrestricted city that boasts more than thirteen cabs for every 1,000 residents (by far the highest ratio in the country), the fare for a typical four-mile trip is only about $2.75. By comparison, in New York City, where notoriously restrictive entry regulations hold the ratio to 1.7 cabs per 1,000 residents, the same trip would cost about $4.75. With high fares translating into high taxi medallion values ($65,000 or more in New York City), it is clear that the costs of monopoly privileges are being passed on to consumers.

Studies have found travelers to be more sensitive to the ready availability of taxis than to speed, comfort, or virtually any other service feature. Not only do cities with open cab entry have more than three times more cabs per capita than regulated ones, but services are often more closely integrated with local bus and rail services as well. Taxis have also proven their strength in low-density residential areas where public transit is highly unprofitable or uncompetitive. And in cities where individual owner-operators of cabs are allowed to ply their trade, marginal markets abandoned by large fleets and franchises are again being served.

Experiments with entry and fare deregulation in twenty-two U.S. cities over the past five years have proven quite successful. According to a recent Federal Trade Commission report, the number of firms and cab service hours have risen markedly since deregulation.[1] Moreover, fares have essentially remained unchanged (in inflation-adjusted dollars) and service quality has generally improved (in particular, shorter waits, fewer nonresponses to phone requests, and cleaner vehicles). Deregulation has been a particular boon to small taxi companies and to private individuals who were previously denied entrepreneurial

73

freedom. Significantly, it has also increased employment opportunities for some urban residents, particularly among low-income and minority populations where joblessness is the highest.

Shared-Ride Services. In recent years, governments have been quite solicitous of car pools but have generally been reluctant to extend the ride-sharing concept to taxis by allowing them to pick up more than one party. Shared-ride taxis flourished in Washington, D.C., during World War II, when cab drivers displayed destination signs in their front windows and folks along the route would hail the cabs going their way. Riders got a break in fares, and scarce wartime resources were efficiently used. In 1974, Washington again adopted a version of ride-sharing, primarily in response to gasoline shortages.

To protect passengers against being overcharged when drivers deviate from a route to drop off other customers, a shared-ride system requires zoned fares rather than distance-metered ones. But for the system to work well, it is not necessary that all cabs operate on a shared-ride basis. Since some passengers would prefer to avoid even the modest delays caused when the cab picks up other fares, a mix of exclusive-ride and shared-ride taxis is the best way to satisfy the riding public's preferences.

Many cities already have public ride-sharing, in the form of governmentally subsidized dial-a-ride vans that provide curb-to-curb services for the elderly and handicapped. But demonstration projects in El Cajon, California, Davenport, Iowa, and some twenty other cities reveal that shared-ride taxis can provide the same sort of service at a much lower cost per passenger than these vans, largely because their drivers earn less (even though they carry more customers). In most of these places, a travel voucher program gives senior citizens, disabled persons, and poorer persons a choice of whether to travel by bus, shared-ride taxi, or dial-a-van. These user subsidies have proven to be an efficient way to underwrite the travel expenses of disadvantaged persons while also promoting healthy competition among different service-providers.

Perhaps surprisingly, shared-ride taxis have also turned out to be a blessing to local bus systems. Not only do they feed passengers to bus lines and rail stations, they also siphon off some of the peak demand. This "peak-load shedding," as it is called, can result in real cost savings to public transit. Past studies consistently show that it costs two to three times more to run buses during rush hours than at other times, largely because restrictive union work rules require that drivers be paid time-and-a-half if they work during both the morning and evening peak. In Singapore, the program that limits the numbers and types of vehicles entering the downtown area during the daytime relies heavily on shared-ride taxis to absorb many of the displaced auto passengers, thus holding the public transit system to a much more manageable scale. In short, by supplementing bus runs at peak hours and serving senior citizens and disabled persons at other hours, a system of shared-ride taxis makes it possible to use vehicles more efficiently throughout the entire day.

Jitneys. Jitneys extend the shared-ride concept by carrying up to a dozen passengers, usually in a station wagon, over a semi-fixed route on a fairly regular basis. Typically the operator picks up customers until the vehicle is full and makes only slight detours from a major street. Popular early in this century, jitneys were banned in most cities around World War I, victims of the trolley-operators' charge of "cream skimming" and unfair competition. Though jitneys may well have threatened city transit systems in 1920, a time when those systems were in their infancy and struggling to survive, they would actually benefit urban transit systems today by providing, as shared-ride taxis do, a much-needed supplement to peak-period capacity.

In many Latin American, Asian, and Middle Eastern cities, jitneys are the chief mode of urban transportation. It has been estimated, for instance, that they accommodate over half of the daily travelers in Caracas, Buenos Aires, and Istanbul. They are also enjoying a comeback of sorts in this country. Jitneys now operate legally in San Francisco, Atlantic City, and most recently San Diego, although local ordinances hold their numbers below 500 even in these places. And in Chicago, Pittsburgh, Baton Rouge, Miami, Chattanooga, and probably other cities as well, jitney services are in such great demand that drivers operate illegally. In Chattanooga alone, over eighty-five illegal jitneys serve 2 million willing customers a year. These clandestine operations generally thrive in low-income, minority communities where there is a demand for a hybrid service—half taxi, half bus. Authorities have tended to look the other way when confronting these illegal, yet successful, operations.

Recent Experiments with Taxi and Jitney Deregulation. Seattle, San Diego, and Portland (Oregon) virtually eliminated their restrictions on taxis and shared-ride services in 1979. All three either removed the ceiling on taxi permits or raised it significantly and, in addition, permitted ride-sharing in taxis and allowed exclusive-ride fares to vary. (The shared-ride services were priced on a zoned basis, except in Seattle, which retained metered rates with adjustments to prevent cabbies from penalizing customers when picking up extra fares.) San

75

Diego legalized jitneys as well. Although taxi operators and the transit interests fought to preserve their entrenched positions in all three cities, strong city council and public support for reform ultimately prevailed.

By late 1983, the total number of taxi permits had increased by 128 percent in San Diego, 30 percent in Seattle, and around 12 percent in Portland. In all cities, there are now many more small cab companies and private owner-operators than before. In Seattle, for instance, the number of small fleets (those with four to thirteen cabs) rose from nine to twenty-three, whereas the share of cabs held by the three largest firms declined from 70 to 54 percent. More cabs have meant more service. Total weekly service in San Diego, for example, measured by cab hours of service, has increased 26 percent since deregulation. Decontrol has also led to greater market specialization, with the smaller and newer operators concentrating on hail and long-haul business and the larger and older companies going after the phone-request and package delivery business. Passenger waits at major cabstands have virtually disappeared in all three places. Average waits for San Diego's radio-dispatched cabs, moreover, fell from 10 to 8 minutes in the first two years of deregulation. In Seattle, price decontrol has also led to a variety of fare structures, including off-peak discounts and cut rates for repeat, advance-reservation customers.

The experience with legalized jitneys in San Diego has been equally impressive. By early 1983 fifteen jitney companies, owning a total of forty-eight licensed vehicles and serving nearly 12,000 weekly customers, had entered the market. They operate on streets paralleling the new light-rail trolley system and main bus routes, concentrating mainly on commercial strips, military bases, and tourist spots, such as hotels and airports. San Diego's jitneys and shared-ride taxis can set any rates they want, up to a maximum, so long as they post them in two-inch lettering in the front window. Fares have proven to be a real bargain. A five-mile trip from airport to downtown San Diego, for instance, today costs around $3 by jitney compared with $12 by exclusive-ride taxi.

In all three cities, the only major snag with deregulation to date has been isolated instances of price-gouging, especially at airports where tourists not accustomed to deregulated taxi fares were easy prey.[2] All three responded by imposing fare ceilings on airport cabs. Also in 1983, San Diego, prompted largely by the bad press generated by the airport incidents, placed a one-year moratorium on new taxi permits to give the city council time to reassess the entire program. Overall, however, residents and visitors in all three cities have materially benefited from the specialization of services and the lower real prices made possible by deregulation.

Deregulating Van Pools and Commuter Buses

Van pools and commuter buses—the paratransit modes that provide prearranged or book-in-advance commuting—have also been stifled by regulation, though perhaps to a lesser extent than taxis and jitneys. In the 1970s, when van pools first became popular, a number of state courts ruled that they were public carriers and thus subject to various certification requirements. Some even interpreted van pools as illegal bus lines. More recently, several state legislatures, notably California's and Tennessee's, have exempted employer-sponsored vehicles that carry fifteen or fewer passengers from state regulation. All states permit voluntary, share-the-expense car pools, while most prohibit van services that are not related to employment and operate for profit.

Commuter buses are providing increasing numbers of subscribers with comfortable express service between their home communities and offices in a number of cities. Typically, however, commuter bus operators must prove their services are necessary and in the public interest before they may begin service. Even in the Los Angeles area, where the country's largest fleet of subscription buses carries over 5,000 daily commuters to work in comfort, transit authorities have succeeded in holding the number of runs below market demand. A recent study by the Southern California Association of Governments found that the Los Angeles area could save over $5 million a year by allowing subscription buses, which operate at about half the cost of public transit, to replace twenty-two local bus routes. Yet transit authorities have filed protests against a number of commuter bus applications.

In 1982 Tennessee passed a law that could provide a useful model for relaxing controls on private bus operations. Within certain counties designated as "citizen transportation areas," Tennessee's public service commission now permits ordinary private vehicles to offer passenger services. Church and other special purpose buses are doubling as commuter vehicles in these counties. These reforms have provided vital travel alternatives to residents of small communities that have recently lost intercity bus services.

Deregulating Parking

Another way to improve urban transportation conditions would be to relax zoning ordinances that require developers of new buildings to provide off-street parking. Typically, these ordinances mandate a minimum number of parking spaces per dwelling unit or per square foot of office space, the purpose being to ensure that traffic coming to a particular site can be adequately handled. The assumption seems to be that a certain number of workers "need" to travel by auto. Therefore, ample space must be provided.

But parking ordinances present a number of problems. First, since they are in effect a tax on the quantity of floor space in a new building, they distort land markets. Indeed, this distortion may be increasing. Parking demand has declined with the rise in fuel costs and the switch to smaller cars—so that now, according to the Urban Land Institute, most shopping center developers will settle for up to 18 percent fewer spaces than heretofore. Yet most cities have been slow to modify their zoning ordinances in recognition of these factors.

Moreover, there is a somewhat disquieting "rule-of-thumb" air about many of these ordinances: some require much more parking than the private market would provide on its own, while others require less. One study, for instance, found that in California minimum parking-space requirements for a 10,000 square-foot office building vary from ten in Long Beach to eighty in Placentia. Moreover, local planning departments often bargain for more than the minimum number of spaces in negotiating with private developers, resulting in even greater variation in the supply of parking for comparable types of buildings and developments.

Third, by making parking artificially abundant, the ordinances have made it harder for public transit to compete for customers. Past evidence has generally proven that parking supply influences the travel modes people choose more than reductions in transit fares or increases in the frequency of bus service. In fact, it has become a standard axiom among urban transportation professionals that auto *disincentives*, such as parking bans, will relieve traffic congestion far more effectively than any assortment of public transit *incentives*. Furthermore, parking regulations may shift new development away from the built-up areas where public transit is competitive and toward lower-density areas where land for parking lots can be bought more cheaply. Thus, allowing developers to reduce on-site parking would strengthen transit systems in a second way: new development would be closer in as well as denser.

Recently, Seattle, San Francisco, and Portland (Oregon) have all lifted minimum parking requirements for new downtown developments. The total number of parking spaces has dropped by 2 percent in downtown Seattle since the late seventies, even as thirteen major new projects were being built. Other cities are reducing or eliminating off-street parking requirements for developers who agree to support transit or ride-sharing programs for their tenants. In both Los Angeles and Palo Alto, California, builders provide "effective alternatives to auto access," such as van pool leasing and cash payments to transit agencies, again in return for less stringent parking requirements.

Other Candidates for Reform

A number of other regulations hamper progress in the urban transportation sector as well. Most American communities, for example, place a lid on the allowable density of various types of land uses, the purpose being to comply with regional land-use goals and to ensure that excessive demands are not placed on local sewer, water, and road facilities. In addition, suburban governments generally encourage the provision of ample roadway capacity and off-street parking, often as a precondition to approving a new subdivision. Local planners also tend to recommend that a planned subdivision be made less dense whenever studies suggest the project will generate more traffic than the nearby roads and intersections can handle.

The problem with this low-density bias is that it precludes the development of the customer base needed to support public transit and ride-sharing alternatives to the automobile. Modifying local ordinances to allow public officials greater flexibility in setting residential densities could prove to be a tremendous inducement to better transit over the long run.

Finally, controls having perverse effects on urban transportation have also come from the federal level. In particular, the federal government has directly contributed to transit's financial dilemma through various requirements (often tied to subsidy programs) that effectively increase the costs of local transit services. Most notably, section 13(c) of the amended Urban Mass Transportation Act of 1964 provides that transit employees must not be adversely affected by any program involving federal grants. This stipulation has been blamed for encouraging overly generous wage settlements by giving labor a virtual veto power over federal transit grants. Section 13(c) has also helped unions secure contract clauses that guarantee workers forty hours a week pay even if they actually work less and that prohibit the hiring of part-time employees. Moreover, 13(c) has been used to keep public transit's competitors out of the market. In Norfolk, Virginia, for instance, unions sued under 13(c) when the local transit agency turned unproductive routes over to a private dial-a-ride operator.

Similarly, the Davis-Bacon Act, which requires that the prevailing wage level (in practice, union wages) be paid on federally funded construction projects, has also increased costs. Two of the best-known recent instances of this are the rapid rail systems of Washington, D.C., and Atlanta. With labor expenses accounting for roughly 70 percent of the cost of operating most U.S. transit systems, the fiscal consequences of these laws have been substantial.

Overcoming Resistance

Regulations governing urban transportation have been built up, layer by layer, to the point where they are now a major barrier to innovation. Reform is needed to create a freely competitve transportation marketplace in our cities.

Admittedly, however, deregulation could have some adverse effects. For one, certain groups might suffer, particularly if public transit services were replaced by paratransit on a wholesale scale. A shift toward high quality services priced at premium fares might be expected to increase travel options for affluent residents while perhaps diminishing them for poorer city residents. It is also possible that some carriers might pursue exclusionary practices and some cabbies might refuse to serve minority neighborhoods. To date, however, there is no evidence that that is happening in cities where taxis have been deregulated. Moreover, the fare reductions that result from taxi deregulation can be expected to benefit the poor most, because they spend a larger share of their income on taxis than other groups. User subsidies could also be introduced to help cover the travel costs of low-income persons. Overall, it would seem more likely that a deregulated environment would offer all Americans, regardless of income, a richer assortment of travel options than they now have.

The relaxation of entry restrictions on taxis and shared-ride services would also impose some inequities on medallion owners, some of whom have paid as much as $65,000 for their licenses. A municipality might buy back all medallions at their purchase price, although that would require a substantial cash outlay. Still, it would make sense to provide some compensation for those who paid the prevailing medallion prices under the previous regime of limited entry.

Decontrol of entry might also undermine transit services along corridors where a natural monopoly exists. However, past research has consistently shown that, with the exception of electrically powered operations (trains and trolleys), most transit services operate under conditions of constant returns to scale. Thus, the natural monopoly argument for regulating entry would seem to have limited application. Surely the benefits of deregulation would on balance far offset any detrimental effects a few transit systems might experience from heavy competition.

In sum, there seem to be very few reasons for imposing price and supply controls on taxis, jitneys, club buses, and parking, and quite a few reasons not to. What is needed, today more than ever, is a freely competitive transportation environment in which the traveling public can enjoy a mix of service and price options. No assortment of technological fixes could do as much as deregulation to relieve congestion, strengthen existing public transit systems, and improve the quality of life in America's central cities.

Notes

1. Federal Trade Commission, "An Economic Analysis of Taxicab Deregulation," May 1984.
2. On the Seattle case, see Richard O. Zerbe, Jr., "Seattle Taxis: Deregulation Hits a Pothole," *Regulation* (November/December 1983), pp. 43–48.

11

Efficiency in Mass Transit: An Inquiry into the Effects of Regulation

Joseph P. Schwieterman

Mass transit is generally considered an exclusive responsibility of the public sector in America. The widespread acceptance of this prevailing view is reflected in extensive state and local regulation that greatly limits private transit initiative in our major metropolitan areas. This regulation not only requires transit entrepreneurs to conduct expensive public hearings before initiating service and to comply with unfavorable pricing and scheduling guidelines, but also requires them to obtain legal permission to operate in the form of certificates of public convenience and necessity. These certificates are typically denied or delayed in the bureaucratic process because of bitter opposition from established operators.

Potential of the Private Sector in Mass Transit

A growing number of scholars are presenting evidence that the private sector can help reverse the falling productivity, rising deficits, and disappointing ridership levels of our urban transit systems, however, and this evidence is bolstering popular support for regulatory reform. The changing political climate, together with the industry's growing financial crisis, has encouraged policy makers to consider dismantling the restrictive route and price regulation that, in many states, has protected the status quo for over fifty years.

Nevertheless, because it has been necessary to rely heavily on the experiences of foreign countries with vastly different socioeconomic factors (such as Great Britain, Singapore, and Thailand) to demonstrate the economic and marketing advantages of the private sector, policy makers have received much of this research with quiet skepticism. Progress has been limited to a few progressive cities and states, and little action has been taken in most major transit-dependent cities. In sharp contrast to other sectors of the transportation industry where America has assumed a leadership role in regulatory reform, the United States has taken comparatively little action to reintroduce the element of competition into the ailing transit industry.

At the center of the prevailing skepticism toward deregulation lies the belief that transit firms enjoy declining marginal costs that can best be exploited under conditions of monopoly. Under this view, private firms are often considered to be little more than costly disruptions in the efforts of public operators to provide cost-effective service, and many are accused of unfairly "skimming the cream" by providing service only during the peak business period.

This skepticism toward the role of the private sector is voiced most vehemently when the public sector has invested heavily in a rail transit system. Fixed-guideway transit systems are characterized by large amounts of immobile assets such as right of way, station facilities, and specialized equipment, and these factors render private sector competition on parallel routes an extremely controversial issue. Many argue that rail transit systems enjoy powerful "economies of density" that can best be exploited through monopolistic protection. This suggests, for example, that a 5 percent ridership loss to private operators will increase per passenger cost of handling the remaining 95 percent, even if appropriate service cutbacks are made.

Furthermore, private sector competition is highly controversial once the public has invested in a rail transit system because public rail operators are often believed to be unable to eliminate the excess capacity in response to ridership shifts to the private sector. Railroad service can be efficiently adjusted only in train-sized increments (simply shortening trains saves little), and this can limit management's ability to respond to small, less-than-train-sized losses in ridership. Many claim that this inevitably leads to increased deficits that ultimately must be financed by taxpayers.

These arguments against private sector participation in transit are questionable at best, as we are learning from a unique sequence of events leading to a dramatic return of the private sector into Chicago's transit market. The Chicago experience solidly demonstrates the growing interest of American entrepreneurs in entering many important but long-monopolized transit markets and provides unprecedented opportunity to challenge the prevailing view that transit is most effectively operated as a government monopoly.

Today, over a hundred privately operated subscription buses, handling nearly 5,000 passengers and operated by a dozen independent charter firms, provide express bus services between central Chicago and its suburbs. Offering monthly "subscriptions" at less than half the price of public rail service, the private operators have quickly established themselves as an important transportation alternative to public rail services for dozens of suburban communities. School bus equipment, part-time labor, and neighborhood bus stops are used to provide consumers with a convenient no-frills service to the city's Loop district. Service can be provided for as little as $.043 per seat mile—a full $.07 less than comparable public rail service.

In sharp contrast to privately operated services in other cities, which appeal primarily to markets poorly served or unserved by public carriers, Chicago's subscription buses are boldly entering into direct competition with heavily subsidized rail carriers. The controversial new service mode is concentrated almost exclusively in the dense Illinois Central Gulf (ICG) rail transit corridor, operates parallel to these heavily subsidized Regional Transportation Authority (RTA) services, and is patronized almost exclusively by former commuter railroad passengers. Not surprisingly, the buses have become the focus of substantial criticism from public transit unions and management.

The ICG rail transit corridor extends south from the city's Loop district to southern suburbs, including Homewood, Flossmoor, and University Park, on a separated, electrified right of way. The financial performance of the service has declined markedly over the past decade, primarily because of rising labor costs. Although train operations regularly broke even only a decade ago, today's trains cover less than 70 percent of their short-term operating costs.

The ICG rail services experience substantial "diseconomies of peaking": highly concentrated demand during the peak periods results in higher costs of providing service. This reflects the large number of transit cars, train crews, and rights of way that the railroad must maintain for use during only a few hours of the day. This peaking problem has dire consequences for utilization of labor; nearly 50 percent of the full-time train crew members are idle for over six hours during the off-peak period. More than 80 percent of the ridership in the corridor occurs during weekday peak periods from 6:40 A.M. to 8:00 A.M. and from 4:20 P.M. to 5:40 P.M. It is during these periods—the periods of greatest costs—that the subscription buses have attracted ridership from the public rail system.

Chicago's subscription buses operate as charter bus services rather than as common carriers, and this arrangement has allowed them to circumvent the complex public transit regulation that, if enforced, would lead to their demise. Lengthy legal processes, coupled with route and price regulation impairing their operational flexibility, would render the services uneconomical in most suburban locations. Because of the dependence of low-income groups on the services, local officials have taken little action except to see that all operators are properly insured.

Economic Implications

As more passengers are attracted from public to private transit services, fewer resources will be needed to support the public services. Trains can be eliminated, equipment retired or sold, labor furloughed, and administrative expenses trimmed. Ultimately, the question to be answered is whether this shift in resources from public to private control is in the best interest of the public: will it lead to a more efficient transit system? The outcome depends heavily on the ability and willingness of the public carrier to divest itself of unneeded services.

Opponents of the private sector in Chicago have argued that labor union contracts, constraints on capital divestiture, and powerful economies of scale render it socially inefficient to allow private operators to capture market share from the publicly subsidized rail system. They claim that public rail transit, like other "public utilities," enjoys declining marginal costs that render competition "destructive."

A study that I conducted through Northwestern University's Transportation Center helps refute these claims through an in-depth evaluation of the cost structure of both the private and the public transit modes.[1] By analyzing and categorizing all relevant expense accounts reported to the Interstate Commerce Commission (in total, seventy-five expense accounts were considered), evaluating important constraints on divestiture such as capital replacement costs and labor law, and conducting ridership surveys, the study simulates the long-run economic implications of a shift in market share to the private sector. The study estimates the consequences of trimming down the size of the public operator in proportion to the growth of the private operator.

Because private sector commuter services in Chicago (and most other cities) are limited to the peak period, their impact on the RTA ridership and costs is similarly limited. My study estimates that the elimination of one round trip by an Illinois Central Gulf train would enable car miles to be reduced by 6 percent and peak car need by 8.8 percent. There will be lengthy lags in realizing many of the cost reductions made possible by these reductions in service; the study used a twenty-year planning horizon.

Estimates of the reductions in car miles, peak car need, and system revenue brought about by ridership shifts to the private sector are used to estimate the potential reductions in cost of the public mode.

To reflect uncertainties in the ability and willingness of the public carrier to eliminate unneeded service, the study examines three scenarios. The first, "complete excess capacity elimination," assumes the public carrier is willing and able to reduce service in direct proportion to ridership losses to the private sector. The second scenario, "partial excess capacity elimination," assumes the public carrier can eliminate service at only half the rate at which ridership is lost to private competitors. The third scenario assumes that no excess capacity is eliminated by the public carrier. Under these three scenarios, specific conclusions have emerged regarding the effects of ridership shifts to the private sector and related public sector cutbacks as they bear on the efficiency of service in the corridor.

The study also projects the consequences of competition from the private sector on RTA deficits and finds that these effects as well depend greatly on the ability of the public sector to divest unneeded services. The shift in market share to the private sector affects the operating efficiency of transit in the corridor (measured in cost per seat mile), depending on which excess capacity scenario is used. Consequently, it was necessary to conduct a ridership survey of all rush hour trains to determine which scenario for the elimination of excess capacity is most appropriate. It was found that, despite the claim of many transit officials, the elimination of *all* excess capacity is both a feasible and an attractive economic option. Our ridership survey illustrates that it is possible for the public transit operator to eliminate as many as three six-car, double-decked electric trains each rush hour because of the ridership loss to private competitors. This constitutes an 18 percent reduction in available seat miles each peak period. (Such calculations were instrumental in refuting claims made by the public transit agency that service cutbacks were operationally infeasible.)

These service reductions can be translated into cost savings, even considering the highly liberal provisions for severance pay to all furloughed employees (six full years for many unionized rail workers) and costly time lags in realizing savings from capital divestiture (depreciation schedules were consulted to make these calculations). If the public transit operator eliminates excess capacity during the peak period in response to the expansion of the competition (as private businesses unquestionably would), the study reveals that the average cost of transit service, public and private combined, would *decline* by more than 5 percent in the corridor. An improvement in operating efficiency of this magnitude equates to a reduction in cost of approximately $1.5 million per year. In sharp contrast to the predictions of the anticompetition lobby, deficits would also be lower under this scenario. Currently, subscription buses are costing the public carrier roughly $2.1 million per year in revenue. If the carrier completely eliminates excess capacity, long-run costs could be reduced by roughly $2.5 million per year. Hence annual deficits could be trimmed by $400,000, or 2 percent.

It is important to note that the efficiency of the public carrier declines slightly under this scenario. This confirms the fact that public railroad systems enjoy economies of density—a factor that must be considered when evaluating the potential role of the private sector. Like other public utilities, the efficiency of RTA services appears to be greatest in the absence of competition. But the expansion of the lower-cost private sector more than offsets this efficiency loss. The overall efficiency of transit in the corridor (both modes combined) improves significantly. This is the relevant measure of the effects of competition on social welfare.

Chicago's RTA has, thus far, not eliminated excess capacity in the corridor in response to subscription bus competition. In the long run, if no service is reduced, the average cost per passenger mile will rise from 11.995 cents to 12.82 cents, and the annual deficit, as noted, will rise by $2.1 million; in the long run, if the RTA continues to resist the elimination of excess capacity this raises serious questions regarding the agency's ability to serve the public.

Some have argued that public rail services are of higher quality than those of private subscription bus services, making cost comparisons unfair. When I make a quality adjustment, however, I find quality differences to be without much analytical significance, and even in the most extreme scenario (weighed heavily in favor of the public transit monopoly), the private sector has a positive effect on net marketplace efficiency.

Conclusions

These are significant findings. They suggest that the "natural monopoly" argument (the public is best served by a single government-regulated transit carrier) is highly dubious in the case of Chicago's transit system. Similarly, accusations that private operators destructively "skim the cream" are not supported.

The Chicago experience, though only one example, is an important case that deregulation advocates can use in demonstrating the favorable dynamics of a competitive marketplace. It demonstrates that flexible, private transit systems provide a favorable alternative to those operated by regulated government agencies, even when subsidies permit public transit fares to be held artificially low.

Another important implication of the Chicago subscription bus phenomenon is that government should use the presence of the private sector as a basis for strengthening its bargaining position with organized labor and contract carriers. Efforts to modernize work rules, eliminate featherbedding, allow split-shifts, and implement other cost-containment measures should be intensified. Unlike past efforts to attain such reforms (when publicly subsidized rail carriers and organized labor enjoyed a virtual monopoly in the transit marketplace), today's policy makers are in a comparatively stronger position to effect such changes.

Publicly subsidized operators, having a vested interest in maintaining a powerful market position, are likely to oppose these recommendations. The evidence suggests, however, that the most common arguments against private competition are not supported. The conclusion seems clear: dismantling the complex web of transit regulation in our major cities will help improve the operating efficiency of the transit industry by stimulating entrepreneurial initiative and create important opportunities for slimming down our financially ailing public transit systems.

Note

1. The study uses the Simpson and Curtin peak-base cost allocation model to calculate commuter costs during the peak period. This model uses data that are readily available in the Illinois Central Gulf *R-1 Annual Report to the Interstate Commerce Commission*. For further details on the study, see Joseph R. Schwieterman, "Competition in Mass Transit: A Case Study of the Chicago Subscription Bus Phenomenon" (M.S. thesis, Northwestern University, 1983) or the September 1984 issue of *Reason* magazine.

12

What If Transit Markets Were Freed?

George S. Tolley

Contemplating what urban transit would be like in the absence of regulation and subsidies may seem like thinking the unthinkable. In these times when the deregulation movement has brought many industries closer to a free-market situation, few industries—and perhaps none—have been carried as far in the opposite direction, away from a market clearing equilibrium, as the transit industry has.

Failure to allow full adjustment to changes wrought by the automobile accounts in great measure for the present fettered state of transit affairs. In the early 1900s it seemed unthinkable to allow the new-fangled horseless carriages to be used as competition to the streetcars, to follow them along and lure away their passengers. As a result, jitneys were effectively outlawed at the beginning of this century and remain so in most places in this country.

And it seemed unthinkable not to try to keep urban bus and rail traffic going at modest prices after World War II when private automobile ownership increasingly decimated transit ridership. As a result, almost all transit companies were taken over by public agencies. Fares became politicized, and subsidies grew astoundingly.

What would urban transit be like today if left to markets without intervention? Would the outcome be unthinkable? In the sense that it is amenable to objective analysis, the outcome is certainly thinkable. Only if we contemplate the outcome objectively can there be a basis for saying whether freer markets in transit are thinkable or unthinkable, in the sense of having either good or devastating effects or being politically feasible or unfeasible.

David Ranson, Sharon Bruce, Charles Kahn, Anthony Pagano, John Crihfield, and I undertook a study of what urban transit would be like under free-market conditions, and we found the answers to be less obvious than expected. The present chapter reports on the results of our study.[1]

The study used the apparatus of supply and demand in analyzing transit markets, and it applied concepts from welfare economics to estimate gains and losses. Price-response parameters, costs of traveling by different modes, and other data needed to express outcomes in quantitative terms were gleaned to the maximum extent possible from the transportation literature. In many cases the numbers from the literature had to be supplemented with judgments. The results should be viewed as general orders of magnitude rather than as highly precise figures.

Mass Transit

By far the most important cause of departures from free-market conditions in urban transit is the existence of mass transit subsidies to bus and rail lines. In 1980, the year to which all the numbers in the study are keyed, 6.6 billion rides were by mass transit. Transit subsidies amounted to $7.8 billion. Somewhat over half of the subsidies were provided by the federal government, largely as capital grants, and somewhat under half were provided by local and state governments, largely as operating assistance. The subsidies paid for about two-thirds of the costs of bus and rail rides. With the cost of a ride of say $1.75, the taxpayer was paying $1.25 for each ride taken, and the rider was paying about $.50.

Among the several things that would happen if the subsidies were removed, fares would rise. We drew on the 1983 study of Pucher and others on the effects of transit subsidies on wages and costs in the transit industry, which found that subsidies result in higher wages for transit workers on subsidized lines.[2] Using their results, we estimate that wages are raised $500 million a year by transit subsidies, or about $.10 per ride. Another effect of subsidies is inefficiency in transit, which means that transit services are not provided with as few resources as they could be: more worker time and equipment are used to supply a given number of rides than would be used in the absence of subsidies. This effect amounts to $800 million or about $.15 a ride.

Thus $.10 per ride is transferred to workers, and $.15 per ride is lost through waste or sheer inefficiency. As a result, if mass transit subsidies were eliminated, the present $1.75 cost per ride would be reduced by $.25 to a cost of $1.50 per ride, and fares would rise from $.50 to $1.50 per ride.

If an elasticity of demand is applied to the rise in fares, the estimate is that a decrease in ridership of about 1 billion would occur. Total mass transit rides would decrease from 6.6 billion to 5.6 billion. In dollar terms, taxpayers would gain by being relieved of paying the nation's $7.8 billion transit subsidies. Workers would lose the amount by which subsidies raise wages, or $500 million. Riders would lose $6.1 billion. The riders' losses would consist of two parts. First and most important, riders would pay more for the rides that would still be taken. This part of the loss equals $1.00 a ride times the 5.6 billion rides still taken, or $5.6 billion. Second and less important quantitatively, they would lose the value to them of the rides no longer taken, from which must be subtracted the savings from not having to pay for those rides. Based on the consumer surplus approach, this second part of the loss is estimated to be one-half the $1.00 change in price of rides times the 1 billion change in number of rides, or $500 million.

There would be a net gain in efficiency of $1.2 billion. The efficiency gain consists of reductions in resources used in providing rides still taken plus savings of resources over the value of the rides that no longer need to be provided.

When rides are transferred between markets—such as between mass transit and taxi markets—and if the other markets are also not efficient, further gain or loss can occur, as will be dealt with in a later section when relations between markets are considered.

Jitneys

The prohibition of jitneys is the second most important cause of departure from free-market conditions. At present, virtually no jitneys exist in this country, but it is estimated that jitneys would provide 1 billion rides at a fare of $.80 if they were allowed.[3] Riders would experience a gain of benefit over cost averaging $.40 a ride, or $400 million.

Another part of the gain for jitneys comes from the fact that rides would be drawn out of mass transit. Every time a ride is drawn out of mass transit under present conditions, there is an efficiency gain to taxpayers of the difference between the roughly $1.75 the ride costs and the $.50 the rider pays. This gain comes to $450 million.

Lifting the prohibition on jitneys would produce a net or efficiency gain of $850 million, which is the sum of the $400 million excess of value to riders over cost of the jitney rides plus the $450 million efficiency gain from the decline in mass transit rides.

The findings for the major effects of the removal of subsidies on mass transit and jitneys may be combined to obtain an idea of how the face of America would change if we had unfettered transit markets in the cities. The main change is that there would be far less bus and rail transit and far more jitneys. We would be paying about $1.50 for mass transit rides and about $.80 a ride for jitneys. The total number of rides provided by both mass transit and jitneys would be rather similar to what it is now.

Van Pools

Discrimination against van pools takes a number of forms. Most important, van pools in many states are required to adhere to common carrier rules, which are difficult for small operators to conform to. Insurance requirements also raise costs. At least in the past, partial offsets have included the investment tax credit, which reduced the cost of van pooling.

According to our estimates, in the absence of discrimination, about 400 million more van pool rides would be provided at a cost of about $1.20 per trip. The net efficiency loss from the discrimination against van pools is estimated to be $240 million. The cost is borne by potential van pool riders, some of whom are now commuting by transit and some of whom are driving to work in private autos.

Cost-Raising Regulations for Mass Transit

Cost-raising regulations for mass transit are estimated to cost $240 million.[4] The most costly regulations are the safety and service requirements on capital equipment, and the estimate is that these raise capital costs 10 to 15 percent. The amount comes to about $.04 for each mass transit trip taken.

Who loses depends on how fares are affected. A reasonable estimate is that the cost is split about equally between riders and taxpayers. Although the safety requirements raise fares somewhat, they also raise subsidies. Riders are thus estimated to lose $120 million in higher fares because of cost-raising regulations, and taxpayers are estimated to lose $120 million.

Taxi Fare and Entry Restrictions

The efficiency loss from taxi fare and entry restrictions is estimated to be $100 million. Taxis are by far the most difficult form of transit to analyze. Complications are encountered in trying to value waiting time and in determining the effects of taxi regulations on waiting time and on fares. As brought out in the many academic studies of taxi markets, different regulations can have different effects.

The range of estimates of taxi market effects is rather large. The fare-raising effects of medallions provide medallion owners about $50 million a year at the expense of riders. It is estimated that taxi riders lose approximately $150 million because of various restrictions. With medallion owners gaining $50 million, the net or efficiency loss is $100 million.

Further complications have to do with differences between taxi markets, including differences between hailing taxis, waiting at stands, and phoning for them. The nature of the demand for taxis is different in various parts of town. Demand differs by time of day. All these differences are ignored in rules and regulations that impose uniform fare schedules and service standards throughout a political jurisdiction.

The requirement of uniformity cuts down on types and varieties of services offered. If, for example, a uniform fare schedule and uniform service are required, some areas—both high income and low income—are discriminated against. We conjecture that higher quality service would be made available in high-income areas; but in low-income areas lower cost service options would be provided.

Bus Fare and Entry Restrictions

Private buses provided only 6 percent of mass transit rides in 1980. In the fare-setting process, some of the markets are monopolized. A rough estimate is that fares are 10 percent above marginal costs in monopolized markets but 10 percent below marginal costs in other markets. We estimate that taxpayers and riders in these specialized markets lose $50 million, and the owners of private companies gain $25 million. The net or efficiency effect is a $25 million loss.

Cost-Raising Regulations Affecting Taxis

Cost-raising regulations affecting taxis include insurance and safety requirements. They are difficult to evaluate because safety measures and insurance at some level are needed. What is an optimum level of safety requirements? What is an optimum amount of insurance? Our presumption is that the regulations lead to greater than optimum levels, although they may not be much greater. Because most taxi costs are for labor and fuel, the cost effects of safety and insurance regulations are limited. Our rough estimate is that costs are increased by $10 million, with riders losing $8 million and medallion owners losing $2 million.

Conclusion

Because the different markets affect one another, the overall effects are not as straightforward as they might seem. Relations between the markets need to be taken into account.

TABLE 1
Effects of Transportation Measures on Ridership

Transportation Measure	Ridership Effects
Mass transit subsidies	Increase transit rides by over 1 billion Decrease taxi rides by 80 million
Prohibition of jitneys	Decrease jitney rides by 1 billion Increase transit rides by 600 million Increase taxi rides by 400 million
Discrimination against van pools	Decrease van pool rides by 400 million
Cost-raising regulations affecting mass transit	Decrease transit rides by 130 million Increase taxi rides by 9 million
Fare and entry regulations for taxis	Decrease taxi rides by 130 million Increase transit rides by 100 million
Cost-raising regulations affecting taxis	Decrease taxi rides by 10 million
Fare and entry regulations for private buses	Little overall change

Source: Pucher, et al., *Impact of Subsidies.*

Earlier, relations between mass transit and jitneys were considered. For a more comprehensive picture, the combined effects of regulations and subsidies for mass transit, jitneys, and taxis need to be considered. These three forms of transportation are especially closely related. The results of our more extended study of interrelations between these transit markets may be briefly summarized as follows. Eliminating the subsidies in mass transit and the prohibition on jitneys would result in 5.0 billion mass transit rides, as compared with actual transit rides of 6.6 billion. Jitney rides would go from 0 to 1.0 billion rides. For taxis, the elimination of fare and entry restrictions would result in 130 million more taxi rides. Beyond this direct effect of deregulation of taxis, freeing up other transit markets would affect taxis. By the time 400 million taxi rides were lost to jitneys and 80 million were gained from rail and bus transit, there would be a net loss of 189 million taxi rides. Taxis would go from providing a present 2.2 billion rides to about 2.0 billion. Total rides provided by mass transit, jitneys, and taxis combined would be 8.0 billion rides, not too many fewer than the 8.8 billion rides in 1980.

Van pool changes also affect the transit markets. Part of the 400 million–ride increase for van pools would consist of rides formerly provided by mass transit, jitneys, and taxis. The riderships effects of all of the measures considered in the study are summarized in table 1.

The monetary effects on various groups, or distributional effects, are shown in table 2. The cost to taxpayers of all the measures considered in this study is nearly $9 billion. The gains to riders of about $5 billion fall far short of the taxpayer cost. How much riders gain ultimately is moot, however, in view of the possibility that localized transportation advantages increase rents and property values and allow landlords to charge higher rents. Those owning affected properties at the time the subsidies came into effect may be the chief beneficiaries. The $500 million that transit workers gain largely reflects higher pay of the transit workers over those with comparable skills in other jobs. Owners of medallions are benefited by about $50 million and owners of protected private transit companies by about $25 million.

TABLE 2

DISTRIBUTIONAL EFFECTS OF TRANSPORTATION MEASURES

Transportation Measure	Gains and Losses
Mass transit subsidies	Taxpayers lose $7.8 billion Riders gain $6.1 billion Workers gain $500 million
Prohibition of jitneys	Riders lose $400 million Taxpayers lose $450 million from increased transit subsidies
Discrimination against van pools	Riders lose $240 million
Cost-raising regulations affecting mass transit	Riders lose $120 million Taxpayers lose $120 million
Fare and entry regulations for taxis	Riders lose $150 million Medallion owners gain $50 million
Fare and entry regulations for private buses	Taxpayers and riders in specialized markets lose $50 million Owners of protected companies gain $25 million
Cost-raising regulations affecting taxis	Riders lose $8 million Medallion owners lose $2 million

SOURCE: Pucher, et al., *Impact of Subsidies.*

TABLE 3

ECONOMIC EFFICIENCY EFFECTS OF TRANSPORTATION MEASURES

Transportation Measure	Economic Efficiency Loss (dollars)
Mass transit subsidies	1,200 million
Prohibition of jitneys	850 million
Discrimination against van pools	240 million
Cost-raising regulations for mass transit	240 million
Fare and entry regulations for private buses	25 million
Cost-raising regulations for taxis	10 million

SOURCE: Pucher, et al., *Impact of Subsidies.*

The net or economic efficiency effects are given in table 3. The economic efficiency effect for each measure is the difference between the gains and losses of the groups affected by the measure. The ordering of efficiency losses in table 3 reflects the text discussion, with mass transit subsidies and prohibitions of jitneys being the most important. The total over all the measures is a $2.6 billion loss for the economy.

For many people interested in cities, it is unthinkable to reduce mass transit subsidies very much because of the fear that center cities would be disadvantaged as places of employment if commuting were made more costly or infeasible. What would happen to jobs in cities in the absence of transit subsidies? It is not clear that a very different picture of cities would emerge. Although fares now subsidized would be higher, substitute transit would expand. Buses would still serve high-density routes. Service could actually be better in some low-income areas with jitneys feeding those areas more fully. Jobs for jitney operators and others from low-income areas would be provided. Without trying to paint a full picture of what would happen to the cities, if one starts down the road of thinking the unthinkable—freeing up transit markets—one finds a not intractable world.

This study has concentrated on the effects of total deregulation of transit markets. Though this alternative is not necessarily realistic at this time, the study demonstrates the usefulness of thinking more fully about transit in terms of demand and supply and taking account of relations between different markets. The study suggests that it is both feasible and desirable to contemplate a wider range of transit policy options than is usually considered.

Notes

1. G. S. Tolley, R. D. Eckert, S. J. Bruce, and R. D. Ranson, *Regulatory Impediments to Private Sector Transit. Volume II: Assessment and Recommendations.* Prepared for Urban Mass Transit Administration (Boston: H. C. Wainwright and Co., 1984). Unless otherwise noted all the figures reported in the present chapter are from this reference.

2. J. Pucher, A. Martstedt, and I. Hirschman, "Impact of Subsidies on the Cost of Urban Public Transport," *Journal of Transport Economics and Policy,* vol. 17 (May 1983), pp. 155–76.

3. Tolley, et al., *Regulatory Impediments.*

4. Ibid.

Part Six

Foreign Innovations in Public Transit

13
Privatization in British Transport Policy

Sir Alan A. Walters

The main progress in British transport policy is the privatization of urban bus service, throughout the whole of Britain except in London. Why not London? The reason is purely political: London is having its government reorganized. It is felt that the mess caused by reorganizing all these petty barons and their miscellaneous acolytes who rule London will be so upsetting that they are not about to try to divest buses at the same time. Excluding London, then, the whole of the United Kingdom is in the process of gaining deregulated private entry into the bus system. I think it will be substantially privatized, although that is not part of the requirements of the bus bill. Privatization of urban buses is one practical step forward.

I do not see any immediate hope of privatizing the railways, however, although there may be a possibility that smaller lines will be privatized. Those who know London and have the temerity to get on the trains and the resolution to stay on them until the end of the journey know that some railway lines in London probably could be privatized. There have also been many suggestions of lines that could be carved off from British Rail and privatized.

There have been some successes with privatizations of tiny railways. In fact, on little railways here and there where people are invited to become engine drivers, guards, and the like, they will actually pay to do the job. Then the labor costs become negative. (Inside every adult is a little boy who wants to play with trains.) There are three striking examples of this approach, and they make money. But I do not think this augurs any substantial privatization of railways, except, of course, for getting rid of subsidiary services.

In Britain one of the big privatizations is the railway hotels, those imposing Gothic monsters of red brick that greet one at the end of a tiring journey. They have improved considerably with the private ownership.

Privatization of Bus Service

Bus privatization and deregulation are very important elements of the privatization program. And it is not small beer. I was struck by the size of the subsidies: in Britain the subsidy is about £850 million, or about $1.2 billion. To get the relative sizes in the United States with respect to Britain, multiply by approximately seven. The equivalent U.S. figure, then, is about $8 billion. In addition, there are local subsidies that I find quite impossible to trace. These subsidies not only are for urban transport, but also go to other kinds of bus companies. They do not, however, include long-distance coach services, similar to Greyhound and Trailways. Those are excluded.

These long-distance or intercity coaches were deregulated four years ago. The deregulation has been a very considerable success with lower fares and better and more frequent services.

The urban bus system, next on the list, is probably one of the most important measures of privatization of this government. It is even more important in its way than British Telecom, and British Gas.

The next major point relates to the proposals of bus deregulation and privatization that were tried in "experiments." One of the major areas for experiment was in Hereford. The idea was to simulate conditions such as those envisaged in the bus bill—that is, free entry, relaxed fare control, and the like—and observe the results.

The general results of the experiments were quite interesting. Costs went down by about one-third. Services changed, but without any deterioration, so far as one could detect, in the quality of services. Indeed, it was remarked that the bus drivers, instead of stepping on the accelerator when they saw someone running for the bus, would actually stop. That is unusual but not unwelcome behavior for public bus drivers.

There was also a general increase in frequency, as well as a variety of changes in other services. The general result of these experiments suggests, first, that quite big gains could be made by switching to private entry, nonmunicipalized service and, second, that considerable gains would be made by a savings on subsidies.

The savings that emerged from the calculations by the Ministry of Transport were fairly high: it was estimated that costs would decline by about 30 percent.

There was no intention of going to a completely unsubsidized system, because for good political reasons it was recognized that subsidies could not be removed from people who had enjoyed them for many past years. And the subsidies were received partly by labor.

In fact, our estimates suggest a very considerable increase, not so much in wages, though, as in inefficient work practices—particularly the refusal to work split shifts. That is, a man will not work four hours in the morning peak and four hours in the evening peak. If he goes on in the morning at say 6:00 A.M., he works the eight-hour morning shift to 2:00 P.M. One has to hire somebody else for the evening shift. The willingness of private operators to work split shifts was quite a big gain in the pilot cases.

It is impossible to sort out the various parts of the subsidy that were absorbed by the work practices of labor. The efficiency factor, however, becomes very important with the very large buses, those that seat forty and have a standing capacity for eighty. Even without the specific capital subsidy in Britain (as those in the United States have), which gives rise to these monsters, the capital is virtually free for these transport operators. So naturally they use a lot of capital and little labor in their operations.

By the way, this is the sort of thing that the U.S. government severely criticizes in foreign countries. Recipients of aid are slapped over their knuckles for subsidizing capital at the expense of employment. There undoubtedly has been a lot of change in the equipment that is bought. In Britain, we have had these large double-decker buses for the typical bus operator. In many small towns with bridge height restrictions, they operate small buses.

The double-decker buses have to have special equipment for servicing and special garaging, because they are not like little minibuses that can be parked in the lanes behind the house. Drivers have to trundle off to the depots, and everybody has to travel from home to the depots to pick them up, a source of enormous waste. The smaller vehicles do not require these large quantities of capital equipment to service them. Incidentally, I think that explains why the load factors are so very low on these large buses: the buses spend a lot of time on dead running from and to the depot. Even during the peak period in London, the average passenger load per double-decker bus was only about sixteen. Under free entry, we got a considerable increase in the load factor and, in fact, an increase rather than a reduction in the availability of seats on most routes.

These pilot projects were shown to be a considerable success. The pilot projects told us little, however, about the matter that was really uppermost in any minister's mind, the political problems of winning acceptance for privatization. As I mentioned before, ministers envisaged the continuation of subsidies, at least for quite a while.

The political opposition came from the usual quarters, but it came from some unusual quarters, too—such as conservatives who were fearful that they would lose their traditional bus service. It had to be dealt with in some way or another.

Other Privatizations

We have had a lot of experience in privatization now in the United Kingdom. We have made our mistakes and learned from them. I think one of the major worries in privatizing is to see that there is a sufficient constituency in favor of privatization so that it sticks, so that it is not reversed by an incoming Socialist government. It is a good idea, therefore, to incorporate disincentives to renationalization, a so-called poison pill.

There are ways of doing that. One of the most important ways was practiced in the successful privatization of the National Freight Corporation. This was not a transit firm, but was primarily a parcel operation, like United Parcel, together with warehouses and other miscellaneous activities. That public corporation was privatized in 1982 through a management and worker buy-out. The workers who supported this were, of course, members of the trade union. If they have suitable incentives they could much inhibit a renationalization.

The management and workers bought shares at a nominal one pound a share. In 1984 at a shareholders' meeting, according to the accountants who are very conservative, each share was valued at £10 and according to market indicators in early 1987 each share would fetch about £40. So the worker enjoyed a very considerable profit from this privatization. The company had never made a profit before. The growth prospects of that company are now bright, even brilliant. I think it is unlikely to be taken back into public ownership.

The privatization of British Telecom is another interesting case. There one could not envisage a worker buy-out or a management buy-out. It was necessary not merely to induce the workers to buy shares but also to hold them. This was achieved partly through the device of a "fixed price" issue and partly through giving workers in the company an incentive in the form of a bonus issue if they held onto their shares for various longish periods.

Political Complications

There is another political aspect, however, which I ought to have foreseen but did not. This was the reaction of rural areas to the reduction of their traditional bus service—note, not a reduction in their transportation, but in the *large* bus service. Many of the constituents, conservative in the old-fashioned sense, did not want to lose their big buses, notwithstanding the fact that the big buses did not run frequently or the fact that the people who complained most never used the bus.

The people who made the most effective complaints, if I may put it that way, were important people in the Conservative party. Some complained that there would be no buses for the servants.

On these lightly traveled routes, it was therefore decided that subsidies would be continued and bus service would be provided at a given frequency. It decided that the authorities would (invite) a *negative* bid to provide these services, so as to minimize the subsidy for these services. The fare and nature of the service was specified—such as hourly frequency on Sunday and half hour frequency during the other days. The bus operators were then asked to specify the subsidy they would require to operate the service. The (positive) subsidy is then determined by competitive bidding.

The other interesting aspect of the bus bill is that the Conservative government tried to push it through at a particular stage of the political cycle. The election was likely to take place in one year's time and certain to take place before two years' time. Any negative political impact of this, therefore, is likely to be fairly high in the period before the election. The sorting out process, as it did in airline deregulation here—as it does in any deregulation—is always likely to give rise to a few juicy scandals and some horror stories. I think it was quite courageous of the government to put this issue so high on the agenda.

One of the great problems is to answer the question, what will the bus system look like when it is deregulated and privatized? The short answer is that none of us know. Where we have seen deregulation and privatization, we have not been able to predict at all well what the outcome would be. There are all sorts of initiatives that we have not thought about because we are not the custodian of all such knowledge.

Obviously, the consequences of deregulation and privatization cannot be predicted. All that can be said is that at least people have the opportunity to make things better, opportunities that they did not have before.

We have met the argument that because deregulation of entry will still not enable the private operator to turn a profit in competition with the subsidized, publicly owned operator, why deregulate? If no one will enter the market, why do we need the regulation that keeps them out? My simple rule is this: if the regulations are effective, they are bad; if they are ineffective, they are irrelevant. Why have ineffective regulations on the books?

The argument of others was that the public authorities had already tried all the innovations in equipment etc. being entertained by the private sector. It was argued that, in spite of 3 million unemployed in 1983, these capital-intensive methods with their large buses were much the cheapest way to provide services. The regulated industry argued that it had tried small buses and they had failed: nobody wanted to ride them. It is true; but I suspect that these trials were deliberately designed to fail.

Let me give an example. In London one of the regulated minibuses traveled along Bishop's Avenue to Hampstead tube station, an avenue noted more for its millionaires than for its transit users. If I were designing a small bus operation to fail, I would certainly have chosen that route.

I also recall the case in which someone wanted to test minibuses in London by running a service along two bus routes, at no cost to the taxpayer. He was not allowed to do so, and London Transport was one of the main objectors. Nicholas Ridley, the minister of transport, for political reasons had to turn down this application. London Transport regarded this scheme as the thin end of the wedge: so it would have been!

Another experience also involves London Transport. It operated a bus from Harrow, in northwest London, that a London Transport executive wanted to withdraw from service. The locals wanted to keep it and suggested allowing one of the private coach operators to run the route. London Transport was covering only 25 percent of its costs there; its executives believed it was ridiculous to continue the service and predicted failure. In a moment of weakness the London Transport executive was induced to agree that the private coach operator could come in and operate it—and it has been operating for about twelve years, presumably profitably under the same fare structure.

All the indications are that the bus bill will be a very considerable success. It will take some time to settle down, and it may yet get caught up in a political cycle, with all that implies.

In addressing the matter of the estimated savings from the privatization of bus services, I see cost savings of about a third, perhaps considerably more than that. In my comparisons of private and public services in the same city, the average saving was about a half. It was considerably higher in some cities. In Istanbul, for example, the savings were about two-thirds. Indeed, the one-third may well be an underestimate.

The Form of Subsidies

As for the *form* of the subsidy, in Britain we have set our face firmly against a capital subsidy, which is what one observes in the United States. It seems to me that a capital subsidy is quite silly. It wastes capital at the expense of employment. What we wanted was a voucher system, and we explored the possibilities. The most attractive scheme was a voucher system with a secondary market. Bus vouchers would be distributed to the target population. Such vouchers would be accepted by the bus operator and redeemed for cash from the authorities. With a secondary market, those who did not want to use them to travel could sell them to those that do. This voucher scheme was rejected on pseudo-administrative grounds. The administration was said to be very difficult. Problems such as whether the vouchers would be usable only on specific routes gave rise to a great deal of discussion and argument.

The voucher system, then—which I think must be dear to the heart of every economist if we have to subsidize—fell largely on administrative grounds. But there were also political arguments against it. The voucher, for some odd reason, has a bad political press.

Now, there are other forms of subsidy, such as free rides for old-age pensioners, which would not normally be provided, of course, in a private system. Such subsidies would have to be administered through passes with reimbursement. These problems have not been completely solved.

I dwelt on the bus initiative because it does seem to me the biggest step forward in the United Kingdom. There are, however, many other privatization initiatives in progress. For instance, a private airport is now being set up in London Docklands, which is very unusual in Britain. Of course, we are selling off the London airports, again (in my view, wrongly), as a package. Instead we should have split them up and sold them off as competing airports. The government was convinced that we should split the British Airport Authority into components and competing units at privatization. The chairman of the British Airport Authority, however, fought a long campaign against dividing them, to get them all under his wing. He won. It demonstrates the power of the incumbent.

The argument was that if they were split up and sold individually, accounts would have to be split up, which would take many years. The delay was the crucial argument: it would take too long. The bureaucracy has its own way of doing things.

Conclusion

When I gave this talk in June 1986 the deregulation of urban buses was in its infancy. It was not at all clear what would happen. Now some months later, although with a competitive market process one is *never* certain of the evolutionary effects, one can say that the deregulation was an initial success. Perhaps the most important political indicator is that buses are not front-page news. There have been no reports of protesting passengers or of violent pickets. Yet very profound changes are taking place. The minibus has already made substantial penetrations into the market. The demand for minibuses by transport firms has been enormous, and the already declining demand for the standard bus has suffered another cruel twist. Moreover, there are many reports of new firms entering the market and of old firms adapting. But the evidence is so far fragmentary and anecdotal rather than statistical and ubiquitous.

The return of a new Conservative government in 1987—and the leadership of Mrs. Thatcher—suggests that the deregulated privatized bus system is here to stay. For my part, I am confident that the outcome will be good.

14
Private Sector Roles in Urban Public Transport

Gabriel Roth

Preferences of Urban Travelers

Some might consider it appropriate to start a paper on urban transport with a comparison of different options and identification of the most efficient or economical mode. But I have been too long in this business to do any such thing. I am well aware that economy, efficiency, or (heaven forbid!) low cost will not help to make my case. So I shall attempt a different starting point. What mode of public transport would urban travelers prefer as an alternative to single-occupancy motorized vehicles?

To answer this question, it is necessary to describe some of the characteristics of travel in U.S. cities and to ask why more than 90% of motorized trips are made by private automobile rather than by public transport. Commentators frequently attribute the flight from conventional transit to some irrational "love affair with the automobile" and suggest that, if only Americans behaved sensibly, they would switch from private to public transport, at least for the journey to work.

This view is superficial and misleading. People travel to increase the opportunities available to them—that is, opportunities to live in pleasant surroundings, to work for desirable employers, to shop in desirable places, to be entertained, to meet friends, to be educated. As people get richer, they do not, as a rule, use their wealth or rearrange their activities so as to reduce travel; on the contrary, in the United States, as in other societies, travel tends to increase with income. This is illustrated by figure 1, which shows how, in 1977,

This paper was written while the author was on special leave from the World Bank before joining The Services Group, a nonprofit consultancy specializing in the private provision of public services. Neither the World Bank nor The Services Group necessarily endorses the data presented or views expressed in this paper.

FIGURE 1
DISTANCE TRAVELED DAILY PER HOUSEHOLD
COMPARED WITH HOUSEHOLD INCOME IN BALTIMORE, 1977

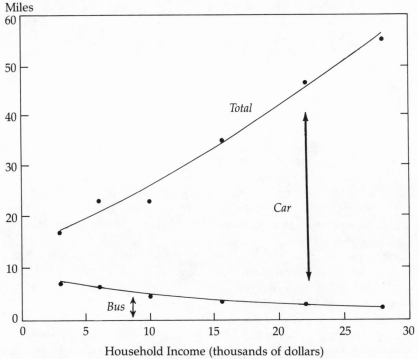

SOURCE: Yacov Zahavi, "Travel Regularities in Baltimore, Washington, London and Reading."

average daily travel distance per household in Baltimore increased as income increased.[1] The increase in total distance traveled was due both to increases in average trip lengths and to increases in the numbers of trips per household.

But how can people increase the distances they travel? One way would be to spend more of their time on travel. But, as people grow richer, their time becomes more valuable and they tend to spend less, rather than more, time on travel. People constrained by a shortage of time—as most of us are—can only increase their travel by traveling faster. And indeed, the Baltimore data (figure 2) show that travel speeds there increased with income.

This was due, of course, to the higher automobile ownership associated with increasing income; and figure 1 shows clearly that the

110

increased travel per household was, on average, due to increased travel by automobile, not by bus.

It is to be expected, then, that as incomes rise in the future—as they are most likely to do—people will tend to seek faster modes of travel to enable them to make the most of the spatial opportunities available to them. Speed is, of course, recognized to be the main factor in the choice of travel mode in both the United States and the rest of the world. It follows, therefore, that the surest way to enable public transport to compete with the private car is to raise its door-to-door speed.

A second key characteristic of American urban dwellers is their desire to live at low density. Some planners disapprove of low-density living and refer to it disparagingly as "sprawl." Despite a significant movement of the childless and the unmarried to city centers, the mainstream of American population movement is still from city cen-

FIGURE 2
SPEED OF TRAVEL COMPARED WITH HOUSEHOLD INCOME
IN BALTIMORE, 1977

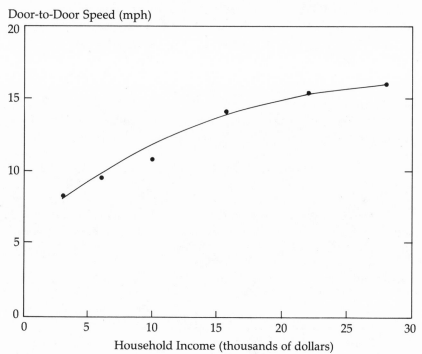

Door-to-Door Speed (mph)

Household Income (thousands of dollars)

SOURCE: Same as figure 1.

ters to suburbs, and from high-density areas (in the Northeast) to low-density ones (in the South and West). But suburban living cannot be efficiently served by fixed-route bus or rail lines: fast door-to-door service in low-density neighborhoods can be provided only by a transport mode flexible enough to arrive quickly close to people's homes in response to their needs.

Let us then, in our pursuit of excellence, consider what would likely be the most desirable form of public transport for low-density American cities, irrespective of cost. The answer might well be shared taxis or minibuses, collecting people from a group of destinations close to one another and traveling nonstop to another group of destinations. Indeed, unless travelers can park at their destinations, a shared taxi or minibus might even provide faster service than a private car. Minibuses and shared taxis can also offer their patrons seats, another characteristic of travel that is given high priority.

But speed cannot be provided by vehicles alone; there is also a need for a suitable "track" or "right-of-way," segregated from the rest of the traffic. Public transport can be speeded up by dedicating to it a reserved right-of-way. This is the primary advantage of the railway and of the "busway." As railway trains cannot provide service away from their track, they cannot satisfy the requirements of both speed and flexibility except in very special situations—for example, on journeys that start and finish in the vicinity of the same railway line. Reserved busways—or bus lanes on highways—are better suited to accommodate flexible public transport services, as they can provide uninterrupted runs over long distances by vehicles that can pick up and set down passengers close to the origins and destinations of their journeys. Such busways, or bus lanes, can accommodate full-sized buses, minibuses, van pools, and even car pools.

Vehicles for Choosy Passengers

The conventional wisdom in North America and Europe is that urban public transport has to be provided by a publicly owned or franchised monopoly and that services have to be slow, congested, and unprofitable. There are numerous examples, however, from cities large and small, rich and poor, of public transport systems that provide high-quality service, without subsidy, at prices that most people can afford.

Minibuses in Hong Kong and Kuala Lumpur. Minibus services in Hong Kong and Kuala Lumpur were introduced to meet needs that the regular services would not satisfy. They have become extremely popular, with the result that the authorities currently limit their numbers to 4,350 in Hong Kong and to 400 in Kuala Lumpur to protect the regular, franchised services. In consequence, the fortunate owners of licenses obtain substantial financial returns from their vehicles.

Route Associations in Buenos Aires and Calcutta. In some cities, individual bus owners form an association to operate a bus route. Each member of the association owns and operates his own bus, while the association has the responsibility of operating a particular route. These associations, which have to compete against other public transport buses, have rules to regularize the relationships between members; for example, buses have to keep to timetables so as not to "steal" customers from preceding and following buses. In Buenos Aires, virtually all city buses are operated by route associations that compete against one another. (Buenos Aires is the only known example of a major city in which bus services were "demunicipalized" and returned to the private sector; the results are generally considered to have been a spectacular success.) In Calcutta, the private operators make enough profit to stay in business, while the public operating company, which charges the same fares and has the best routes, runs at a substantial deficit.

The Jeepneys of Manila. The Jeepney services, which were first operated with surplus U.S. Army jeeps (hence the name "Jeepneys"), offer an alternative service to that provided by the regular bus companies. Jeepneys are generally individually owned, though many are organized in route associations. Fares are similar to those of the regular bus companies, but while the regular bus companies are in financial difficulty, many of the operators of the 28,000 licensed Jeepneys are anxious to get more licenses to expand services.

The *Dolmus* of Istanbul and the Minibuses of Cairo. Similar in principle to the Jeepneys, the *dolmus* have been established in Turkey for many years. Cairo's minibus services have developed recently and rapidly with official encouragement.

School Buses in Singapore. In Singapore, where school buildings are used for separate morning and afternoon shifts, and where neither shift coincides with business hours, school bus operators are empowered to enter into monthly contracts with office workers to take them from home to work on a regular basis. Casual pickup of workers is not allowed under this scheme, which gives each school bus operator six assured trips each day. In addition, there is another service in

113

Singapore, which allows private operators to ply for hire along designated routes, but only in peak periods.

The *Matatu* of Nairobi. These minibuses, similar in some ways to those operating in Hong Kong and Kuala Lumpur, complement the services of the conventional bus company and are particularly important in serving slum areas untouched by the regular service. The government of Kenya, with the help of the World Bank, was planning to establish an agency to finance the purchase of minibuses by private operators with a view to relieving urban unemployment and simultaneously improving public transport.

The *Bakassi* of Khartoum. The *bakassi*, converted Toyota pickup trucks, carry tens of thousands of passengers per day. In mid-1979, 3,300 of them were operating on the crowded streets of Khartoum. Although *bakassi* owners must contend with gas rations and shortages of spare parts, business seems to be successful.

Shared Taxis in Belfast. "Black taxis" are operated by sectarian groups to enable their supporters to travel despite interruptions in the conventional services. They provide quick and low-cost transport, under crowded conditions (up to eight people per shared taxi) and are profitable, though fares are no higher than those charged by the bus company.

The *Publicos* of Puerto Rico. Puerto Rico's *publicos* (shared taxis and minibuses) have been established for many years as a service that offers higher speeds than the bus, at a higher fare. They maintained their financial viability into the 1980s, while the conventional bus system has been unable to cover its costs without subsidy.

Characteristics of Successful Informal Public Transport Systems

The success of the informal systems has been recognized for many years, but the reasons for success were not generally understood. Grava[2] and Walters[3], have, identified four key factors that are associated with this form of public transport:

- ownership is private
- vehicles are small
- operating units are small
- route associations provide effective organizational frameworks

Ownership. That publicly owned bus companies sustain losses is not entirely surprising, as the systems taken over by public authorities tend to be the ones that cannot be run at a profit by private operators. But the large losses under public ownership seem to have little relationship to increases in service levels. The losses appear to be due to the higher cost levels (especially wages) that can be afforded by subsidized systems and the inability of publicly owned operators to resist pressures from politicians to hold down fares and expand unremunerative services. Evidence from Australia, where public and private bus companies operate in similar conditions, shows that the costs of the former exceed those of the latter by some 50 percent.[4]

Size of Vehicle. One of the established (but questionable) principles of public transport operation is that large vehicles are more economical to operate than small ones. The reason given is that, with over two-thirds of bus operating costs being due to labor, it pays a bus company to have large vehicles, even if they are full for only a fraction of their working lives, so as to avoid the additional labor costs that would be required to meet peak demand with small vehicles. This reasoning, though perfectly logical, may be questioned on two grounds.

The first is that the capital cost *per seat* seems to increase with the size of the vehicle. Operators in San Juan, Puerto Rico, for example, can expect to pay $17,000 for a minibus seating seventeen, but $140,000 for a full-sized bus seating fifty. Thus a full-sized bus can cost almost three times as much per unit of passenger capacity as a minibus. (Incidentally, the same pattern is evident when moving up to a rail car: a vehicle seating, say, 150 passengers, can easily cost $1 million.) The main reason is that small vehicles such as minibuses can be mass produced and bought "off the shelf," while large ones tend to be made to special order and are assembled as separate units.

A second reason favoring the small bus, while more subtle, may be more important. For a given route capacity, small buses provide more frequent service than large ones and therefore involve less waiting time per passenger. This factor might not matter to a franchised operator who has to bear the costs of his crew but not the waiting time of his customers; hence the preference of monopoly operators for big vehicles. Where competition is allowed, however, those who provide public transport have to respond to the needs of the passengers, most of whom dislike waiting for buses. To reduce waiting it is necessary to use small vehicles providing a frequent service. It is significant that when the private bus operators took over the municipal service in Buenos Aires in 1962 one of their first actions was to replace the large municipal buses with smaller ones. More generally, whenever a private operator has the freedom to choose the size of his vehicle he generally chooses something less than a full-sized bus. The small bus has other advantages: as it holds fewer passengers, it is easier to fill with people starting at one point and wishing to travel to another, so it tends to stop less frequently, and for shorter periods, than large buses; and, being more maneuverable, it can often make its way more quickly along congested roads.

Size of Operating Unit. There is much evidence that large bus fleets incur financial losses under the same conditions that small operators—owner-drivers—make profits. Although operators the world over are reluctant to admit to making profits, the pressures to obtain permits to provide service and the prices at which permits in some cities change hands (or are hired out) are sure indications of profitability.

The reasons for the financial viability of the small transport firm, be it a mover, a taxi driver, or a bus operator, are well known and typical of other types of small business in the service sector. The owner will be willing to work longer and less regular hours than would a paid bus driver in a large fleet. The owner will clean his own vehicle or enlist the help of family members. He will appreciate the need for regular vehicle maintenance. He will not have his own depot but will service his vehicle on the street or at a local garage. His recordkeeping will be minimal. He will make a greater effort than a paid driver to collect fares from passengers and to ensure that the amounts collected do not get lost on the way. An extra driver can be employed if two shifts a day are needed. Some facilities, such as two-way radio service, can add to earnings without the owner's relinquishing control of his vehicle.[5]

In passenger transport, the basic operating unit is the vehicle, and, as the taxi business proves, it is possible for the owner of only one vehicle to operate it successfully at a profit. Indeed, evidence from cities in Asia and Latin America suggests that it is possible for a group of people to own a small bus and to operate it at a profit.

The Route Association. A high level of service over a wide area can be provided by small firms, as long as the organizational structure of the industry is appropriate. Taxis are a case in point. Although some may be operated as one-man (or one-woman) firms and some in large fleets, there is no need for any formal coordination to achieve an acceptable level of service.

The individual unit does, however, have to work within an appropriate organizational framework. A taxi looking for business, for example, has to be recognized by the public as being available for hire. If it is a vehicle intended to carry more than one person, its destination has to be clearly indicated. It is also important for the passenger to know the fare that is being charged and the places at which vehicles can be readily found. Some of these features are provided by route associations, which are located in many cities in Asia, Africa, and Latin America and in some parts of the United States and Europe.

Where route associations exist, the driving and maintenance of each vehicle remain under the control of its owner or owners. What is shared is the route; that is, the members of the association ply a specified route, in conjunction with others, thus offering travelers a frequent service. Fares are generally fixed by the association, but not invariably: In Hong Kong and Istanbul, for example, higher fares are charged in peak periods when demand is higher and traffic congestion more acute (a similar system obtains for Washington, D.C., taxis, which are allowed to charge higher fares in peak periods than in off-peak ones). The revenues in some associations are retained by the individual members, and in others (New Jersey, for example), pooled among the members.

Applications in the United States. Similar systems also operate in the United States. Shared cars—known as "jitneys"—provided public transport successfully in many U.S. cities from 1916 until they were (almost) regulated out of existence in the early 1920s.[6] Some still operate today in Atlantic City, Chicago, San Francisco, and other urban areas. Other high-quality, nonsubsidized, public transport systems in the United States include car pools, van pools, commuter clubs, and subscription bus services. It is obvious that, given the opportunity for profit, the private sector can provide vehicles for passengers; but can it provide the track, or right-of-way, on which the vehicles can travel?

Private Provision of Public Transport Right-of-Way

Unlike the public sector, which can rely on the inexhaustible purse of government to meet losses, the private sector cannot operate without profit. In order to provide infrastructure, it has to be paid. That it can respond to commercial stimulus may be seen from the private urban rail lines that were provided in numerous cities in the nineteenth century. The first such line is reported to have been established in New York in 1832, for horse-drawn omnibuses. Horse transport was slow and environmentally polluting, however, so the private sector made many attempts to replace the horse with mechanical power. One solution was to use steam trains on separate rights-of-way; in 1863 underground steam trains were run in London, and in 1868 similar equipment was used in New York at an elevated level. In all these cases, the owners of the track controlled the vehicles that ran on them, and were remunerated from the fares paid by passengers. And when, in the 1880s, electric streetcars were perfected, they were installed all over the world.

It was not only for trains and streetcars that the private sector provided such infrastructure. In the 1960s a bus operator, Momin Motors in Dhaka, provided a road about seven miles long for its buses. As in the case of the train operators, the road was paid for out of the fares paid by travelers in the company's vehicles. The company was able to get paid for its investment by virtue of its private ownership of the franchise and the vehicles. This road has since been absorbed in the highway network of Bangladesh, but its construction provides a vivid illustration of the private provision of a "public service" even under the most difficult circumstances.

Fixed Rail versus Busways. Mention of the Dhaka busway prompts the question: Why do so many Americans take for granted that "rapid transit" has to be *rail* rapid transit? Busways can be built under or above ground; can provide seated passenger capacity as great as can be provided by railways, often at lower cost. Their capabilities were described by Martin Wohl (currently professor at Carnegie-Mellon University, and a recognized expert on transit) in a formal evaluation of the Washington Metro proposal prepared for the secretary of commerce. He wrote:

> It should be emphasized that such an express bus operation is not in any respect comparable to the present-day bus operation on city streets; rather it would be a rapid transit operation just as free of congestion and traffic delays as a rapid rail transit system, and would differ from a rail transit system only in terms of manner of operation and vehicle size and form. Whereas a rail transit vehicle is restricted to operating on its private rights-of-way, the bus can operate both on its private rights-of-way and on suburban city streets for picking up passengers. The bus can operate in a downtown subway just as rail transit vehicles can. And, furthermore, the general cost analysis conducted by the Rand Corporation indicates that express bus service, operating on private grade-separated rights-of-way on the line haul radials and downtown subways, and operating as suburban feeder buses

on residential area city streets, *will provide faster overall trip speeds and travel times at lower cost than will rapid rail transit.* (Emphasis in original.)

The reasons for stressing the importance of considering other types of technologies, and particularly small vehicle transport, are many and compelling. The first reason is that the service (or replacement) lives of small vehicles are shorter, thus making it possible for them to take advantage of improvements in power, vehicle, or control/guidance units at less cost than for systems of longer life. (Buses have replacement lives in the range of 10 to 15 years, whereas rail transit trains have lives in the range of 25 to 35 years.)

Secondly, with a smaller unit vehicle capacity, bus service can be more nearly "tailored" to meet demand; also, if the same amount of capacity is to be provided, buses will provide such with higher frequency than rail transit trains.[7]

Busways operate successfully in New York (on the exclusive lane of I-495 leading to the New York bus terminal) and on the Shirley Highway leading to Washington, D.C. In both cases there is no shortage of capacity; in fact, there are not enough buses to justify either facility's being dedicated to buses alone all day. The New York busway operates only in the morning peak period, and the Shirley Highway busway admits car pools.

There are not many busways overseas, but one is currently being built in Ottawa. According to Van Wilkins,[8] the system already approved will comprise twenty-two miles of two-lane roadway and is scheduled for completion by 1991. The system will have twenty-six stations, at which the roadway widens to four lanes, allowing some buses to stop without delaying others. Some buses will travel the full length of the busway (or "transitway," to give it its formal title), but others will enter at ramps and run as expresses.

Diesel buses were selected over light rail primarily on the basis of costs, it having been determined that a "light rail" system would have cost about 50 percent more than a system of busways, and its annual operating costs would have been 20 percent higher. A further fact favoring the diesel buses was that they made possible the avoidance of bus-to-rail transfers which, it was calculated, would drive as many patrons back to their cars as a doubling of fares. The routings are designed to enable the buses to circulate through suburban areas to pick up riders and then enter the busway for a fast run to the town center.

The Inter-American Bank has just made a loan to Trinidad, partly to lengthen and improve the busway leading to Port of Spain. A feature worthy of note is that this busway was built on a railway right-of-way. There must be hundreds of miles of abandoned urban railway lines in the United States—such as the one on Atlantic Avenue in Brooklyn—that would be suitable for conversion to busways. Could such conversions be made attractive to private financers?

Private Financing of Urban Busways. The fundamental problem is that urban road space, however congested, is provided to road users without extra charge, except for fuel and tire taxes, which are quite inadequate to cover the costs arising from the use of congested urban roads. To charge public transport vehicles for using their "track," while relieving private cars of having to pay for theirs, makes neither political nor economic sense. Furthermore, the charging of conventional tolls is expensive in both time and money. But if busway users are not charged, how can a private busway provider be remunerated?

One way might be for the authorities to pay "shadow tolls"—that is, amounts appropriate to different classes of traffic—and proportional to the number of vehicles in each class. There is an obvious case for the road owner's being paid *at least* the Highway Trust Fund revenues "earned" on the busway. Under this system, the number of vehicles (or passengers) using the busway would be determined from regular or sample counts. If such payments were insufficient to attract private capital, they could be supplemented by a lump sum, or by annual subventions, the exact amount being determined by a bidding process. To return to the Atlantic Avenue example: The authorities responsible for transport in Brooklyn could invite bids from private firms to convert a six-mile disused railway to a busway. They would offer to pay the private entrepreneur an agreed amount for each passenger or passenger-mile (or for each vehicle or vehicle-mile) and would give the contract to the person or group who would supply the facility according to the design prepared by the authority at the least cost. Maintenance would be the responsibility of the private supplier who would, incidentally, suffer financially if poor maintenance cut down use of the busway. The busway would be open to all buses and minibuses and (if there was spare capacity) possibly to car pools or other high-occupancy vehicles.

Conclusion

It may be concluded, on the basis of evidence from both within and without the United States, that the private sector, where it is allowed to, can provide public transport vehicles more responsive to users' needs, and at less cost, than can be provided by the public sector. The provision of urban road space is more difficult for the private sector, because of the difficulty of charging for it. But it is possible to envisage busways provided by the private sector if appropriate financing mechanisms were designed, for example, public authorities could pay the busway providers at rates appropriate to the vehicle classes using the busway and in proportion to the number of vehicles in each class.

Notes

1. Yacov Zahavi, "Travel Regularities in Baltimore, Washington, London and Reading." Technical Memorandum attached to Progress Report No. 8 on the UMOT Travel Model, presented to the U.S. Department of Transportation, Research and Special Programs Administration, Washington, D.C., 1982.

2. Sigurd Grava, "Locally Generated Transportation Modes of the Developing World," in "Urban Transportation Economics—Special Report 181," Washington, D.C.: National Academy of Sciences, Transportation Research Board, 1978, pp. 84–95.

3. A. A. Walters, "Costs and Scale of Bus Services," World Bank Staff Working Paper No. 325, Washington, D.C., 1979.

4. I. Wallis, "Private Bus Operation in Urban Areas—Their Economics and Roles." R. Travers Morgan Pty., Ltd., Australia, 1979.

5. R. F. Amos, "Shared Taxis in Belfast," PTRC Annual Meeting, Summer 1978.

6. Ross Eckert and George Hilton, "The Jitneys," *Journal of Law and Economics* (October 1972).

7. Martin Wohl, "Evaluation of U.S. National Capital Transportation Agency Report," Report to Executive Office of the President, and Office of Science and Technology, 1963, pp. 90–91.

8. Van Wilkins, "Rapid No Rail," *Bus World*, vol. 6, no. 2, Winter 1985–1986.

Index

125

A Note on the Book

This book was edited by
Janet Schilling and Dana Lane of the
Publications Staff of the American Enterprise Institute.
The figures were drawn by Hördur Karlsson,
and the index was prepared by Julia Petrakis.
The text was set in Palatino, a typeface designed by Hermann Zapf.
Coghill Book Typesetting Company of Richmond, Virginia,
set the type, and Edwards Brothers Incorporated,
of Ann Arbor, Michigan, printed and bound the book,
using permanent, acid-free paper.